Malcolm Shuttleworth
Besseres Englisch

Malcolm Shuttleworth

Besseres Englisch

Die 250 häufigsten Fehler

und wie man sie vermeidet

Anaconda

Many thanks to Sharon Grimbley and Louise Shuttleworth
for their invaluable help.

Die Deutsche Nationalbibliothek verzeichnet diese Publikation in der Deutschen Nationalbibliografie; detaillierte bibliografische Daten sind im Internet unter http://dnb.d-nb.de abrufbar.

Umschlagmotiv: shutterstock.com/Vadim Georgiev
Umschlaggestaltung: Nicole Babel, Köln, www.BABELgum.de
Satz und Layout: Roland Poferl Print-Design, Köln
Printed in Czech Republic 2014
ISBN 978-3-7306-0143-3
www.anacondaverlag.de
info@anacondaverlag.de

Inhalt

1. Must or had to?

Wrong *Last night I must go to bed at nine o'clock.*
Right *Last night I **had to** go to bed at nine o'clock.*

Erklärung

Die Vergangenheitsform von **‚must'** ist **‚had to'**. **‚must'** ist das Gleiche wie **‚have to'**. Dabei ist **‚had to'** die Vergangenheitsform für beide. **‚must'** und **‚have to'** werden für die Gegenwart oder die Zukunft verwendet, **‚had to'** für die Vergangenheit. **‚has to'** wird in der Gegenwart für die dritte Person Singular verwendet (‚he/she/it').

Practice makes perfect

Fill in the gaps using 'must', 'had to' or 'have to', as in the example.

*Yesterday I **had to** go to bed at nine.*

1. *I ____________ go to the doctor's tomorrow.*
2. *John ____________ give up his job because of ill health.*
3. *My mum __________ cook for ten people when she was young.*
4. *I __________ remember to water my plants.*
5. *I __________ go now, bye!*

2. See you

Wrong *We see us tomorrow.*
Right ***See you** tomorrow.*

Erklärung

‚We see us tomorrow' ist ein klassisches Beispiel von Germisch – Deutsch, das direkt ins Englische übersetzt wurde. Richtig ist immer nur **‚see you'**.
Mit **‚see you tomorrow'** kann man auch eine Gruppe von 20 Personen verabschieden.
Man kann auch ein Reflexivpronomen benutzen, wenn sich zwei Personen voneinander verabschieden:

*We'll see **each** other tomorrow.*

Practice makes perfect

Fill in the gaps to complete the sentences, as in the example.

***See you** on Tuesday, bye.*

1. *I'll __________ on Wednesday at seven.*
2. *Sue and Alan won't see __________ for six months.*
3. *We hadn't ______________ since school.*
4. *Have you seen _____________ in the mirror?*
5. *I'm going on holiday tomorrow, _________ in a couple of weeks.*

3. Near

Wrong *I live in the near of London.*
Right *I live **near** London.*

Erklärung

Achtung, Germisch! ‚in der Nähe von' ist nicht gleich ‚in the near of', sondern einfach nur **‚near'** + Ort – also denk dran: Niemals Wort für Wort übersetzen!
Ähnlich, aber nicht dasselbe sind auch **‚near'** und **‚nearby'**:

*I live **near** Cologne. (nämlich ‚in der Nähe von' Köln)*
*I live in Leverkusen, Cologne is **nearby**. (nämlich ‚in der Nähe' ohne nachfolgende Ortsnennung)*

Practice makes perfect

Fill in the gaps to complete the sentences, as in the example.

*I live **near** a church, there is also a mosque **nearby**.*

1. *I live __________ Jim.*
2. *My new flat is great, there are a lot of shops _________.*
3. *How ________ are you to the school?*
4. *There are quite a few restaurants ______ the office.*
5. *Paul moved because he wanted to be ______ his parents.*

4. By myself or by my own?

Wrong *I did the decorating by my own.*
Right *I did the decorating **myself/by myself/on my own**.*

Erklärung

Es gibt nur die Ausdrücke **‚(by) myself'** und **‚on my own'**. Der Ausdruck ‚by my own' existiert nicht.
Alle drei Ausdrücke **‚oneself'**, **‚by oneself'** und **‚on one's own'** können ‚allein, selbstständig, ohne fremde Hilfe' bedeuten:

*Paul did all the work **himself/by himself/on his own.***
(NICHT: alone)

Die Formen lauten: ‚(by) myself/yourself/himself/herself/itself/ourselves/yourselves/themselves' und ‚on my/your/his/her/its/our/your/their own'.
Die beiden Ausdrücke **‚by oneself'** und **‚on one's own'** bedeuten außerdem ‚allein, einsam':

*When I saw Paul, he was **by himself/on his own/alone.***
(allein, kein anderer da)

Practice makes perfect

Complete the sentences by filling in the gaps, using the information above.

1. *I was* ______________ *all night.*
2. *Joe didn't need any help, he did it* ___________.
3. *My mum is very lonely, she is always* _________.
4. *They did it* ________________.
5. *We did it* _________________.

5. Which or who?

Wrong *I hate people which tell lies.*
Right *I hate people **who** tell lies.*

Erklärung

‚**which**' wird immer für Dinge verwendet:
*A fridge is something **which** everyone needs.*
*A stethoscope is something **which** a doctor needs.*
‚**who**' wird immer für Menschen verwendet:
*A thief is someone **who** steals things.*
*A doctor is someone **who** you go to when you're sick.*

Practice makes perfect

Fill in the gaps using 'which' or 'who', as in the example.

*I didn't know **which** one to choose.*

1. *Do you know someone ________ can repair my car?*
2. *John knows someone _________ got sent to prison.*
3. *My mum has a washing machine _______ is always breaking down.*
4. *I was talking to someone ______ remembers you from school.*
5. *I have a bike ______ I don't need.*

6. A friend of you or yours?

Wrong *Is he a friend of you?*
Right *Is he* ***a friend of yours****?*

Erklärung

Ein weiterer häufiger Fehler! Wie im Deutschen benötigt man in diesen Fällen ein besitzanzeigendes Fürwort (mein, dein etc.). Spricht man über Freunde, braucht man zusätzlich ein **‚s'**:

A friend of yours/ours/hers/his/theirs.

Aber Achtung:

A friend of ***mine****.*

Practice makes perfect

Fill in the gaps to complete the sentences.

He seemed to know her, is he a friend of ***hers****?*

1. *Is he a friend of ______?*
2. *Sue said she's bringing a friend of _______ to the party on Friday.*
3. *We bumped into a friend of _______ in London.*
4. *A good friend of ________ had an accident on Sunday.*
5. *They said he was a friend of _________, but I didn't believe them.*

7. Life or live?

Wrong *Do you watch a lot of life music?*
Right *Do you watch a lot of* ***live*** *music?*

Erklärung

‚live' wird auf zwei verschiedene Arten ausgesprochen und hat auch zwei Bedeutungen:

Do you ***live*** *in Germany?*
Do your children still ***live*** *at home?*
(Verb: leben – Aussprache: liv)
The band are playing ***live****.*
The match will be broadcast ***live****.*
(Adjektiv: im Moment des Geschehens – Aussprache: laiv)

‚life' ist das Substantiv (Leben – Aussprache: laif – Plural: **lives**) und wird verwendet, um über Dinge zu sprechen, die Tag für Tag passieren:

My ***life*** *is very complicated at the moment.*
She has a comfortable ***life****.*
That's ***life****!*

Practice makes perfect

Fill in the gaps using 'life' or 'live' in the correct form, as in the example.

The band weren't playing ***live****, it was playback!*

1. *I _______ in Spain.*
2. *Where do you _______?*
3. *This game is coming to you ______ from Wembley.*
4. *Will there be _______ music?*
5. *The lifeboat saved many _________.*

8. Information or an information?

Wrong *Can you send me an information?*
Right *Can you send me (some) information?*

Erklärung

Viele Fehler entstehen, wenn ein Artikel (**‚a/an'**) benutzt wird, obwohl er nicht nötig ist. Die Artikel **‚a/an'** werden nur für zählbare Substantiven in der Einzahl verwendet, also für Dinge, die man zählen kann und die in der Mehrzahl ein **‚s'** am Ende tragen:

*shop**s**, chip**s**, hand**s**, finger**s**, sister**s**, etc.*

Unzählbare Dinge brauchen keinen Artikel, daher:

information – *NICHT: an information*
knowledge – *NICHT: a knowledge*
weather – *NICHT: a weather usw.*

Practice makes perfect

Decide if the following sentences are right or wrong, correct them if necessary.

1. *Jill has a nice furniture in her office.*

2. *We had a great weather on holiday.*

3. *There's an information about the meeting on the noticeboard.*

4. *He has a lot of knowledge about Russia.*

5. *I had a terrible traffic on the way here.*

9. Make or do?

Wrong *He makes a great job.*
Right *He **does** a great job.*

Erklärung

‚**make**' und ‚**do**' werden oft verwechselt. ‚**do**' wird für die meisten täglichen Aktivitäten verwendet:

*What did you **do** today?*
*Are you **doing** well at school?*
*Did you find time to **do** your housework?*

‚**do**' wird auch verwendet, um arbeitsbezogenen Aktivitäten zu beschreiben:

*She **does** a great job.*
*He **does** his homework on Sunday.*
*I **did** the gardening yesterday.*
*I **did** the report you wanted.*

‚***make***' wird verwendet, wenn etwas produziert oder erschaffen wird:

*I've **made** a cake.*
*He **made** a sandwich*
*Sally is **making** a pizza, it smells great!*

Practice makes perfect

Fill in the gaps using 'make' or 'do' in the right form.

1. *John is ________ his homework.*
2. *Have you ________ your French homework yet?*
3. *Did you ________ those candles yourself?*
4. *Who is ________ so much noise?*
5. *I hope he ________ the right thing.*

10. Disappointed or disappointing?

Wrong *He was really disappointing with his exam results.*
Right *He was really **disappointed** with his exam results.*

Erklärung

Adjektive mit **‚ing‘** an Ende beschreiben, wie etwas ist:
*Science is **boring**.*
*Football is **exciting**.*
*The weather is **disappointing**.*
Adjektive mit **‚ed‘** am Ende sagen uns, wie jemand etwas empfindet:
*He is really **excited** about the trip.*
*Sue is totally **bored** with her job.*
*Harry was really **embarrassed** about his behavior.*

Practice makes perfect

Choose the correct word to finish the sentences.

*The concert will be **exciting**/~~excited~~.*

1. *I think he is really fascinating/fascinated.*
2. *The meeting was really bored/boring.*
3. *Sometimes my brother's behavior can be really embarrassed/embarrassing.*
4. *My job can be very tired/tiring.*
5. *Are you interested/interesting in politics?*

11. Trip or travel?

Wrong *How was your travel to Asia?*
Right *How was your **trip** to Asia?*

Erklärung

‚**(to) travel**‘ ist ein Verb und wird für Ferien, Ausflüge und Reisen im Allgemeinen benutzt:

__Travelling__ is one of my hobbies.
*I like to **travel** alone.*
*Does your wife **travel** light?*

‚**trip**‘ bezeichnet den einzelnen Ausflug oder die Ausflüge:

*Did you enjoy your **trip** to Berlin?*

Practice makes perfect

Fill in the gaps using ‘travel’ or ‘trip’.

1. *How many ________ to Cuba is that now?*
2. *Diane likes to ___________ all over the world.*
3. *The _______ agent chose a great hotel for us!*
4. *It was a four-hour _______ from the airport to the hotel.*
5. *My _______ to Rome has been cancelled.*

12. Own or an own?

Wrong *We have an own house.*
Right *We have **our own** house.*

Erklärung

‚We have an own house' ist direkt aus dem Deutschen übersetzt und leider völlig falsch! Will man sagen, dass jemand etwas besitzt, wird ein Possessivpronomen (‚my/your/his/her/its/our/their') + ‚own' benutzt:

*I have **my own** company.*
*He has all **his own** teeth.*
*They have **their own** swimming pool.*

Practice makes perfect

Fill in the gaps to complete the sentences.

1. *I'll have ______ house by the time I'm 30.*

2. *The dog has got ______ basket.*

3. *I can pay for ________ drinks, thank you.*

4. *Did he steal that coat? No, it's _______.*

5. *I can't believe you have _________ flat in Spain!*

13. Five year or years?

Wrong *Steve got a five-years contract.*
Right *Steve got **a five-year** contract.*

Erklärung

Wenn ein Substantiv mit einer Zahl verwendet wird, um ein Adjektiv zu bilden, braucht man kein **'s'** am Ende:

*A hotel has five stars, but it's a **five-star** hotel.*
*The little girl is ten years old, but she is a **ten-year-old** girl.*

Das **'s'** fällt in diesem Fall weg, weil bei der Verbindung von Substantiv und Zahl ein neues Adjektiv entsteht.

Practice makes perfect

Fill in the gaps to complete the sentences.

1. *John has a 10-_______-old daughter.*
2. *The hotel we stayed at had five _______.*
3. *He was jailed for 10 ________.*
4. *The prisoner was given a five-_______ sentence.*
5. *It's a 10-_________ drive into the city.*

14. So much or many?

Wrong *I have so much advantages in my new job.*
Right *I have **so many** advantages in my new job.*

Erklärung

‚many‘ wird für zählbare Dinge verwendet. Die meisten Wörter mit ‚s‘ am Ende sind zählbar:

*windows, chairs, desks – **how many**?*

‚much‘ wird für unzählbare Dinge verwendet, z. B. solche, die man nicht sehen kann oder die nur schwer zu zählen sind:

***too much** imagination, **too much** oxygen, **too much** time*

Oder solche, die tatsächlich unzählbar sind:

*water, sand, coffee – **how much**?*

Auch Dinge mit verschiedenen Formen und Größen sind in der Regel unzählbar:

***too much** traffic, **too much** furniture, **too much** money, etc.*

Practice makes perfect

Fill in the gaps using 'much' or 'many'.

1. *I have so ______ to tell you.*
2. *John spends too ______ money on his car.*
3. *How ______ knowledge do you have about computers?*
4. *I don't know ______ people in this town.*
5. *Her job is just getting too ______ for her.*

15. Spend or donate?

Wrong *He spends a lot of money to charity.*
Right *He **donates** a lot of money to charity.*

Erklärung

‚spend' wird häufig mit dem deutschen Wort ‚spenden' verwechselt:

***Spend** your money **on** fashion, **on** your kids, **on** holidays, etc. (Geld ausgeben)*

***Donate** money **to** charity or good causes. (spenden)*

Practice makes perfect

Fill in the gaps using 'spend' or 'donate' in the correct form.

1. *Did you ______ money to Oxfam again this year?*

2. *Rick ______ all his bonus on a new car.*

3. *How much did you ________ on Christmas presents this year?*

4. *He doesn't like _________ money, he's tight!*

5. *I ___________ € 50 to Save the Children last week.*

16. For or since?

Wrong *I have been here since four hours.*
Right *I have been here **for** four hours.*

Erklärung

Die erste Regel lautet: ‚**for**' + Zeitraum:
__for__ 20 minutes?
__for__ 10 hours?
__for__ a long, long time
__for__ 25 years
Die zweite Regel lautet: ‚**since**' + Zeitpunkt (in der Vergangenheit):
*I've been here **since** three o'clock.*
*I've lived here **since** 1989.*
*I've known John **since** we were kids.*

Practice makes perfect

Fill in the gaps using 'for' or 'since'.

1. *I haven't seen him ______ we left school.*
2. *I've worked for this company ______ 12 years.*
3. *______ when have you been interested in science?*
4. *I've known her ______ over 30 years.*
5. *They have been keeping me waiting _____ three.*

17. Ride, travel or drive?

Wrong *I drove with the train this morning.*
Right *I **travelled by** train this morning.*

Erklärung

‚**(to) ride**' heißt ‚auf etwas sitzen':
(to) ride a bike, a horse or a pony, (to) ride a motorbike or scooter
‚**(to) ride**' wird auch benutzt, wenn man irgendwo einsteigen muss:
(to) ride the train or the bus
Wenn man selbst am Steuer sitzt, verwendet man ‚**(to) drive**':
*(to) **drive** a car*
ABER:
You don't **drive** the bus or the taxi, leave that to the **drivers**!
‚**(to) travel**' heißt ‚reisen', also:
***(to) travel** to Spain*
***(to) travel by** or **with** public transport*
Auf Englisch kann man zur Arbeit ‚reisen':
*Roy **travels** to work **by** bus.*
*She **travels** to work **with** the train.*

Practice makes perfect

Fill in the gaps using 'ride' or 'travel' or 'drive in the correct form.

1. *I like ______ by train, it's less stressful than taking the car.*
2. *She ________ all the way from Frankfurt to Bonn in four hours.*
3. *__________ by taxi is really expensive these days.*
4. *How often do you ________ your bike to work?*
5. *_____________ by public transport is getting more and more expensive.*

250 Fehler

18. At, on or in?

Wrong *I usually read books at the evening.*
Right *I usually read books **in** the evening.*

Erklärung

Zeitangaben und ihre Präpositionen sind oft ein Problem. Hier die Grundlagen!

'on' bei einem bestimmten Tag oder Datum:
__on__ Monday, __on__ the 25th

'at' zu einer bestimmten Zeit
__at__ seven o'clock, __at__ night

'in' bei Zeitangaben wie einem Monat oder Jahr:
__in__ June, __in__ 2011

'in' in Verbindung mit einer bestimmten Tageszeit:
__in__ the morning, __in__ the afternoon, __in__ the evening

Nicht vergessen:
__in__ the morning, but __on__ Saturday morning

Practice makes perfect

Fill in the gaps using 'on', 'in' or 'at'.

1. *I'm meeting Sue ____ Saturday morning.*

2. *Harry always goes for a run ___ the morning.*

3. *My birthday is ____ June.*

4. *My party starts ______ eight.*

5. *They met in Paris ____ 2001.*

19. Do or commit?

Wrong *He did a crime and was sent to prison.*
Right *He **committed** a crime and was sent to prison.*

Erklärung

‚**(to) do**' ist ein sehr allgemeiner Begriff, um irgendeine Handlung zu beschreiben:

*(to) **do** some work, **do** jobs, **do** something, **do** nothing*

‚**(to) commit**' wird für Verbrechen verwendet, ähnlich wie im Deutschen ‚Verbrechen' mit ‚begehen' steht:

*He **committed** a crime, he **committed** a burglary, she **committed** murder.*
*She **committed** suicide. (She killed herself.)*

Practice makes perfect

Fill in the gaps using 'do' or 'commit'.

1. *If you __________ a crime you could get sent to jail.*
2. *Most murders are __________ in the home.*
3. *She couldn't take any more, so she __________ suicide.*
4. *He said he didn't __________ it, but the judge decided he had __________ the crime.*
5. *The burglary was __________ by two brothers.*

20. Prove or proof?

Wrong *The police know he did it, but they can't proof it.*
Right *The police know he did it, but they can't **prove** it.*

Erklärung

‚**(to) prove**' ist das Verb (beweisen):
*I can **prove** it.*
*He **proved** he could do the job.*
*He has **proven** he can do the job.*
‚**proof**' ist das Substantiv (der Beweis):
*We have **proof**.*

Practice makes perfect

Fill in the gaps using 'prove' or 'proof'.

1. *I know he did it, but I have no ______.*
2. *He's guilty, but I can't ______ it.*
3. *He has ______ that he can do the job.*
4. *He admitted it! What more ______ do you need?*
5. *You think I'm a liar? ________ it!*

21. The world

Wrong *It's the biggest country on the world.*
Right *It's the biggest country **in** the world.*

Erklärung

Präpositionen verursachen auch hier manchmal Probleme und es gibt mehrere Möglichkeiten ‚die Welt' in einen Satz einzubauen. **‚on'** steht allerdings nie direkt vor ‚the world':

*It's the biggest **in** the world.*
*You can travel **all over** the world.*
*People **of** the world.*
*The four corners **of** the world.*
*News travels **around** the world.*
*You can feel **on top of** the world.*

Practice makes perfect

Decide if these sentences are correct. Correct them if necessary.

1. *After his massage, Phil felt in top of the world.*
2. *This news concerns all the people of the world.*
3. *The travel show reports from the four corners in the world.*
4. *After his retirement he wants to travel around the world.*
5. *It's the biggest lake of the world.*

22. Me, Myself, I?

Wrong *I sometimes ask me why I bother.*
Right *I sometimes ask **myself** why I bother.*

Erklärung

Hier wurde ein Objektpronomen anstelle des korrekten Reflexivpronomens eingesetzt. Die Reflexivpronomen sind:

I – *myself*
you – *yourself*
he – *himself*
her – *herself*
we – *ourselves*
they – *themselves*
it – *itself*

Practice makes perfect

Fill in the gaps using reflexive pronouns.

1. *I hate ________ for being so weak.*
2. *When the job was done, they cleaned ________ in the lake.*
3. *Bob bought ________ a new TV.*
4. *Don't worry, I'm sure it will sort ________ out soon.*
5. *Sue hurt ________ in the fall.*

23. Terrible or terribly?

Wrong *The cruise was terrible expensive.*
Right *The cruise was **terribly** expensive.*

Erklärung

Adverbien korrekt zu benutzen ist nicht immer einfach. Sie haben zwei Hauptanwendungen. Stehen sie beim Verb, beschreiben sie näher, wie etwas ausgeführt wird:

*She drives **terribly** (because she's a **terrible** driver).*

Stehen sie beim Adjektiv, beschreiben sie dieses näher (z. B. wie teuer etwas ist):

*It's expensive – it's **terribly** expensive.*
*It's cheap – it's **extremely** cheap.*
*It's cold – it's **fiercely** cold.*

Practice makes perfect

Describe the words on the left using an adjective, then describe the adjective using an adverb, as in the example.

bread *Bread is **cheap**.* *Bread is **reasonably cheap**.*

1. *Christmas* ______________________ ______________________
2. *a cream cake* ______________________ ______________________
3. *champagne* ______________________ ______________________
4. *a good friend* ______________________ ______________________
5. *children* ______________________ ______________________

24. At or to?

Wrong *I was on a great festival at the weekend.*
Right *I was* ***at*** *a great festival at the weekend.*

Erklärung

Hat man in der Vergangenheit eine Veranstaltung besucht, benutzt man dafür **‚at'**:

I was ***at*** *a great concert last week.*
I was ***at*** *a great party on Friday.*
Last week I was ***at*** *a seminar*
How did it go ***at*** *the meeting?*

‚to' hingegen wird verwendet, wenn es um die Zukunft geht:

Are you going ***to*** *the conference next week?*

Practice makes perfect

Make sentences using the following words, as in the example.

party – meeting – training course – concert – wedding

I'm going ***to*** *my friend's wedding soon.*

1. ____.
2. ____.
3. ____.
4. ____.
5. ____.

25. Good or well?

Wrong *Helen does her job really good.*
Right *Helen does her job really **well**.*

Erklärung

‚good' ist ein Adjektiv und wird verwendet, um Substantive zu beschreiben:

*The **food** is **good**.*
*My **team** are **good**.*
*His **French** is **good**.*

‚well' ist das Adverb und wird verwendet, um Verben zu beschreiben:

*She **cooks** really **well**.*
*My team **played well**.*
*He **speaks** French really **well**.*

Practice makes perfect

Fill in the gaps using 'good' or 'well'.

1. *I couldn't understand him, his English wasn't very ______.*
2. *Rick did _______ in his final exams.*
3. *I play piano, but I'm not very _____.*
4. *Her performance was very _____.*
5. *Her job is going _____.*

26. Him or it?

Wrong *Clean the cup and put him in the cupboard.*
Right *Clean the cup and put **it** in the cupboard.*

Erklärung

‚it' und **‚him'** sind manchmal problematisch, weil sie **‚es'** und **‚ihm'** sehr ähnlich sind.
‚him' kann nur für Lebewesen benutzt werden. Dies sind vor allem Menschen, nur unter bestimmten Umständen auch Tiere – in der Regel Haustiere:

*What shall I do with the dog? – Put **him** in the yard.*
(Man kann auch sagen: Put it in the yard.)
*Where's Phil?'– I don't know I haven't seen **him***

‚it' wird für unbelebte Objekte benutzt:

*What shall I do with the rest of this pizza? – Put **it** in the fridge.*
*Do you want the rest of this ice-cream? – No, throw **it** in the bin!*

Practice makes perfect

Decide if the sentences are right or wrong. Correct them if necessary.

1. *How's the soup? Do you like him?* ________
2. *Bob's got a new cat. He's called it Fred.* ________
3. *What's your new boss like? Are you getting on with it?* ________
4. *The bus was late. I waited for him for over an hour.* ________
5. *The dog is barking again. I'm getting really fed up with him!* ________

27. Hear or listen to?

Wrong *Bert always hears music in his car.*
Right *Bert always **listens to** music in his car.*

Erklärung

‚**(to) hear**' und ‚**(to) listen**' werden häufig falsch verwendet, z. B. ‚I hear music in the car' oder ‚I listen music in the car'. Der richtige Ausdruck ist ‚I listen to music in the car'. ‚**(to) hear**' beschreibt ein Hören, das plötzlich einsetzt oder nur kurz andauert. In der Regel ist man in dieser Situation ein passiver und zufälliger Zuhörer:

*You can **hear** music from a passing car.*
*You can **hear** a sudden noise.*
*You can **hear** children playing outside as they pass your window.*

‚**(to) listen to**' hingegen beschreibt das aktive Zuhören, das längere Zeit andauert:

***I listened to** the game on the radio.*
***I listened to** his speech with interest.*
***I listened to** Beethoven's fifth last night.*

Practice makes perfect

Fill in the gaps using 'hear' or 'listen to' in the right form.

1. *I often ___________ audio books in the car.*
2. *I tried shouting to him, but he couldn't ___________ me.*
3. *How often do you ___________ the radio?*
4. *I like to wake up and ___________ the sound of the waves crashing onto the beach.*
5. *He ___________ too much heavy metal!*

28. Normal or normally?

Wrong *He always comes late, that's normally.*
Right *He always comes late, that's **normal**.*

Erklärung

‚normal' ist das Adjektiv und wird verwendet, um einen Zustand zu beschreiben:

*It's **normal** to want kids.*
*The weather is **normal** for this time of year.*
*His temperature is **normal**.*

‚normally' ist das Adverb dazu und wird daher bei Verben verwendet:

*He **normally** comes late.*
*We **normally** celebrate my birthday at home.*
*I don't **normally** eat fish.*

Practice makes perfect

Decide if the sentences are right or wrong, as in the example. Correct them if necessary.

*I **normally** go to the dentist for a check-up once a year.* Right

1. *I hate going to the dentist, that's normally.* ____________
2. *John normal gets up at six.* ____________
3. *He's just a normally kind of person.* ____________
4. *I don't normally drink so much.* ____________
5. *He normally gets a bonus at Christmas.* ____________

29. Tickets or cards?

Wrong *I have three cards for the theatre.*
Right *I have three **tickets** for the theatre.*

Erklärung

Ein berühmter ‚false friend'. Das deutsche Wort ‚Karten' hat zwei Bedeutungen, für die es im Englischen zwei verschiedene Begriffe gibt. Die deutschen Eintrittskarten oder Fahrkarten sind die englischen **‚tickets'**. Grundsätzlich bezahlt man für **‚tickets'** Geld, um irgendeine Leistung zu erhalten.

*You need a **ticket** to get into something: A **ticket** for the theatre.*
*A **ticket** for the football game.*
*You need a **ticket** to travel on public transport: Can I you see your **tickets**, please? There's a **ticket** machine over there.*
*You need a **ticket** to leave your car in the car park.*

‚cards' sind in der Regel Grußkarten, die man an Geburtstagen, Weihnachten, Jubiläen etc. verschickt:

*How many birthday **cards** did you get?*
*Have you sent any Christmas **cards** this year?*

Practice makes perfect

Fill in the gaps using 'ticket' or 'card' in the correct form.

1. *How many ________ do you need for the show?*
2. *I've got a spare ________ for the game tonight, would you like to come?*
3. *Oh no! I've got another parking ________.*
4. *Did you send mum and dad a ________ for their anniversary?*
5. *I had to pay a € 40 fine because I lost my train _______.*

30. We are/there are

Wrong *We are five people in my office.*
Right ***There are** five people in my office.*

Erklärung

‚there are' (‚es gibt') wird immer für Menschen und Zahlen benutzt:
***There are** five people in my office. (Umgangssprachlicher: ‚**there are** five of us' – dies entspricht dem deutschen ‚wir sind zu fünft'.)*
***There were** seven people at the party. (**There were** seven of us.)*
‚we are' ist eine Form des Verbs ‚(to) be' und wird verwendet, um zu beschreiben, was eine Gruppe von Menschen macht oder fühlt:
***We are** waiting for the bus.*
***We are** bored.*

Practice makes perfect

Fill in the gaps to finish the sentences.

1. *How many people came to the meeting?* ______________________________.
2. ______________ *waiting to hear if we still have jobs.*
3. ______________ *eleven casualties in the crash.*
4. *How many people work in your office?* ______________________________.
5. ______________ *seven people who wanted the job.*

31. Person or persons?

Wrong *10 persons are waiting to see the doctor.*
Right *10 **people** are waiting to see the doctor.*

Erklärung

‚one **person**, several **people**' ist die allgemeine Regel:

*He's a **person** I can do business with.*

*20 **people** are working on the project.*

‚persons' kann im Plural verwendet werden, aber nur in offiziellem Kontext (in Verträgen, von der Polizei oder anderen Beamten):

*This lift can hold up to 10 **persons**.*

*Police are looking for a person or **persons** unknown in connection with the robbery.*

Practice makes perfect

Fill in the gaps using 'person' or 'people'.

1. *How many ________ went to the party?*
2. *He is not a very nice ________.*
3. *I want every ________ in the company to get a bonus.*
4. *Some ________ don't know when to stop.*
5. *She's not very good with ________.*

32. Political or politically?

Wrong *He is not very political correct.*
Right *He is not very **politically** correct.*

Erklärung

Will man ein Adjektiv näher beschreiben, ist es wichtig, daran zu denken, ein Adverb zu verwenden:

*It's correct – it's **politically** correct.*
*He's friendly – he's **environmentally** friendly.*
*It's cheap – it's **extremely** cheap.*
*It's pointless – it's **totally** pointless.*

Practice makes perfect

Describe the following things using an adjective and an adverb. Use the example to help you.

a broken fridge *A broken fridge is totally useless.*

1. *a safe job* ______________________________
2. *a riot* ______________________________
3. *a romantic film* ______________________________
4. *a new-born baby* ______________________________
5. *a day off* ______________________________

33. Dart or darts?

Wrong *Every Friday he plays dart in the pub.*
Right *Every Friday he plays* ***darts*** *in the pub.*

Erklärung

‚darts‘ ist der Name des Spiels. **‚a dart‘** ist das, was man auf die Dartscheibe wirft. Viele Fehler werden gemacht, weil das **‚s‘** am Ende bestimmter Wörter vergessen wird:
Es heißt **‚congratulations‘** (NICHT: ‚congratulation‘).
Es heißt **‚last orders‘** (NICHT: ‚last order‘).
Nicht vergessen: Auch bei der Formulierung ‚einer von vielen‘ (‚one of ***many***‘), muss ein ‚s‘ verwendet werden:

*one of my brother**s***
*one of my teacher**s***
*one of my friend**s***

Practice makes perfect

Decide if the sentences are right or wrong, as in the example. Correct them if necessary.

There's Mr. Jones, he's one of my teacher. Wrong – ***teachers***

1. *He threw a dart at the dartboard.* ____________
2. *One of my friend is getting married next week.* ____________
3. *Some teacher don't know what they are doing.* ____________
4. *It's last order, let me get another round.* ____________
5. *One of my responsibility at work is to answer the phone.* ____________

34. Invest or investment?

Wrong *They are not building the new factory because the invest is too high.*
Right *They are not building the new factory because **the investment** is too high.*

Erklärung

‚(to) invest' ist das Verb – etwas, das man tut. **‚investment'** ist das Substantiv – etwas, das ist. Verben und Substantive darf man nicht verwechseln:

*They **produce** goods in the **production** department.*
*They **invest** a lot of money, because **investment** is important for the future.*
*He was **introduced** to the workers, the manager made the **introductions**.*

Practice makes perfect

Choose the correct word to finish the sentences.

*You have to **register**/~~registration~~ first.*

1. *My brother-in-law is in the building/build trade.*
2. *Producing/production is down by 25%.*
3. *Steve has founded/foundation his own company.*
4. *We have to negotiation/negotiate a new contract.*
5. *That's his fourteenth invention/invent.*

35. Terrible English or a terrible English?

Wrong *He speaks a terrible English.*
Right *He speaks* ***terrible*** *English.*

Erklärung

Unzählbare Dinge brauchen keinen unbestimmten Artikel. Dinge wie Wetter, Geld, Englisch und Französisch werden als unzählbar eingestuft, daher können diese Worte alleine benutzt werden:

We had ***great weather*** *in France.*
Do you need ***money****?*
He speaks wonderful ***English****.*
She speaks awful ***French****.*

Practice makes perfect

Use the following words to make sentences.

1. water/ ______________________________

2. sand/ ______________________________

3. pencil/ ______________________________

4. meeting/ ______________________________

5. money/ ______________________________

36. By or until?

Wrong *I need a reply until tomorrow.*
Right *I need a reply* ***by*** *tomorrow.*

Erklärung

‚by' wird für Fristen verwendet (bis wann etwas geschehen sein muss):

We need the goods ***by*** *Friday.*

We have to make a decision ***by*** *the end of the month.*

Benutze **‚until'**, um auszudrücken, wie viel länger etwas noch dauern wird (wie viel Zeit verstreichen wird, bevor etwas Neues oder anderes passieren kann):

You'll have to wait ***until*** *Friday.*

Bob won't be finished ***until*** *nine.*

I will wait for you ***until*** *seven.*

This film goes on ***until*** *twelve o'clock.*

Practice makes perfect

Choose the correct word ('by/until') to finish the sentences.

1. *I need those figures ________ Friday.*
2. *Can you make sure you are here ________ six?*
3. *We have to leave for the airport ________ nine.*
4. *I waited ________ four, then I went home.*
5. *She was gone ________ the time I got there.*

37. Is or are?

Wrong *The pensions is not so high in my country.*
Right *The pensions **are** not so high in my country.*

Erklärung

Pass auf deine Pluralformen auf!

*My **pension is** too low.*

*The **pensions** in this country **are** too low.*

Andere Beispiele:

*The **staff are** satisfied. (**several** people)*

*My favourite **subjects are** maths and science. (**two** things)*

*Some **words are** hard to pronounce. (**many** words)*

Practice makes perfect

Choose the correct word ('is/are') to finish the sentences.

1. *Germans _______ highly educated.*
2. *Plurals _______ hard to understand.*
3. *Part-time jobs _______ badly paid.*
4. *Knowledge _______ power.*
5. *Weather forecasts _______ sometimes misleading.*

38. I am or I have been?

Wrong *I am in this job for one year now.*
Right ***I have been doing** this job for one year now.*

Erklärung

‚have been doing' oder ***‚has been doing'*** (‚present perfect progressive') beschreiben Zeiträume. Damit wird gesagt, wie lange jemand etwas schon macht – solange diese Handlung noch ausgeführt wird:

> ***I've been writing** this book for over a month now, and I'm still writing it! – Roy **has been working** at the shop for nearly four years. I **have been waiting** in the room for over an hour.*

Practice makes perfect

Answer the questions using 'have been', as in the example.

*How long have you been studying? – **I've been studying** for two years.*

1. *How long have you been living in your current home?*

   ____

2. *How long have you been living in this country?*

   ____

3. *How long have you been learning English?*

   ____

4. *How long have you been reading this book?*

   ____

5. *How long have you been working for your present company?*

   ____

39. About or not?

Wrong *We were discussing about the problem.*
Right *We were **discussing** the problem.*

Erklärung

‚(to) discuss‘ oder **‚(to) talk about’** – entweder oder! Beides geht, aber nicht beides geht mit ‚about‘:

*We will **discuss** the problem at the meeting on Wednesday.*
*I'm seeing Sue on Wednesday, we have a lot of things to **discuss**.*
*If you want to **talk about** it, come to my office this afternoon.*
*I think they've been **talking about** me behind my back.*

Practice makes perfect

Finish the sentences using ‘discuss’ or ‘talk about’ in the correct form.

1. *We ____________ the situation, but we couldn't find an answer.*
2. *She ____________ her new boyfriend all night.*
3. *He's boring, all he ____________ is himself.*
4. *Are you ____________ the new budget plans?*
5. *Let's ____________ it when I get home.*

40. Half-time or part-time?

Wrong *I work half-time.*
Right *I work* ***part-time****.*

Erklärung

‚half-time' ist die Pause in der Mitte eines Fußballspiels (Halbzeit):
The ***half-time*** *score is 1-1.*
‚part-time' und **‚full-time'** werden für Jobs verwendet:
He works ***full-time****.*
She works ***part-time*** *because her kids are still at school.*

Practice makes perfect

Choose the correct word to finish the sentences.

1. *How did you lose? You were winning 3-0 at ________.*
2. *The firm doesn't have enough orders, so I'm working ________ at the moment.*
3. *________ jobs are usually badly paid.*
4. *There are five minutes to ________ and I think both teams need a break.*
5. *Looking after children is a ________ job.*

41. Four p.m. or four o'clock p.m.?

Wrong *Four o'clock p.m.*
Right *Four **p.m.***

Erklärung

Es gibt viele Möglichkeiten, um die Zeit zu beschreiben. Aber auch hier sollte man nicht mischen:

four o'clock
four a.m. *(auch möglich: am)*
four p.m. *(auch möglich: pm)*
four *in the morning*
four o'clock *in the afternoon*

Benutze niemals **‚o'clock'** mit **a.m.** oder **p.m.**!

Practice makes perfect

Choose the correct words to finish the sentences.

*You should go to bed before **midnight**/~~midnight p.m.~~*

1. *We have to be there at four/four o'clock a.m.*
2. *They are meeting early in the afternoon at two a.m./two p.m.*
3. *The party went on until four p.m. in the morning/four a.m.*
4. *The concert starts at eight in the afternoon/evening.*
5. *I've set the alarm for six o'clock/six o'clock a.m.*

42. A need of or a need for?

Wrong *There is no need of the product at the moment.*
Right *There is no need **for** the product at the moment.*

Erklärung

‚for' und **‚of'** können verwirrend sein. Wird etwas (nicht) benötigt, benutzt man **‚for'**:

*There is a need **for** something.*
*a demand **for** something*
*a call **for** aid*

Ansonsten wird **‚of'** benutzt:

*You can be proud **of** something/someone.*
*(to) be afraid **of** something*
*(to) be ashamed **of** something/someone*

Practice makes perfect

Finish the sentences using 'of' or 'for'.

1. *There is a huge demand ____ sports cars at the moment.*
2. *I'm sick and tired _____ my job.*
3. *He said he was ashamed ____ himself.*
4. *He shouted at the child, there was no need ____ that!*
5. *You can be very proud ____ what you have achieved.*

43. Good in or good at something?

Wrong *I'm good in that.*
Right *I'm* ***good at*** *that.*

Erklärung

‚good in something' ist eine direkte Übersetzung aus dem Deutschen, die im Englischen ungrammatisch ist. Hier braucht man **‚at'**:

You can be good ***at****/bad* ***at****/not bad* ***at****/terrible* ***at*** *something.*
I'm good ***at*** *English, but terrible* ***at*** *French.*
Bill's not very good ***at*** *looking after himself.*
I'm terrible ***at*** *getting up in the morning.*
I'm not bad ***at*** *cooking.*

Practice makes perfect

Describe your abilities in the following subjects using 'good at/bad at', etc.

1. *languages* ____________________
2. *cooking* ____________________
3. *managing finances* ____________________
4. *saving money* ____________________
5. *talking in public* ____________________

44. Look on or look at?

Wrong *We need to look on the processes closely.*
Right *We need to **look at** the processes closely.*

Erklärung

‚**(to) look at**' bedeutet in diesem Fall, etwas genauer zu untersuchen oder gründlich zu überprüfen:

*We need to **look at** our spending.*
*We need to **look at** the problem.*

‚**(to) look on**' beschreibt ein passives Zuschauen, während etwas passiert oder jemand etwas tut. In diesem Fall ist man ein ‚**onlooker**'.

*The man was beating the dog while a crowd of people **looked on**.*
*The volcano erupted and thousands of people **looked on** as the lava spilled down the mountainside.*

Practice makes perfect

Use 'look at' or 'look on' in the correct form to finish the sentences.

1. *Can you ___________ my car, I think I've got an oil leak.*
2. *We are ___________ ways of reducing costs.*
3. *___________ the state of him!*
4. *He didn't help me out when the trouble started, he just ___________.*
5. *I'm not sure which one you mean, I'll have a ___________ it when I get home.*

45. At or on the moment?

Wrong *On the moment things are going well.*
Right ***At the moment** things are going well.*

Erklärung

‚at‘ sollte immer für Zeiten verwendet werden:
***at** eight o'clock*
***at** noon*
***at** midnight*
***at** the moment*
‚at‘ kann auch für Urlaubszeiträume verwendet werden:
***at** Christmas*
***at** Easter*
***at** Whitsuntide'(Pfingsten)*
ABER:
***on** a particular day*

Practice makes perfect

Answer the following questions using 'at' or 'on'.

1. *When do you get cards?* ________________________
2. *When do kids get presents?* ________________________
3. *When do they have chocolate eggs in the shops?* ________________________
4. *When do people let off fireworks?* ________________________
5. *When do owls come out?* ________________________

46. Serious or seriously?

Wrong *It's a seriously idea.*
Right *It's a **serious** idea.*

Erklärung

Die Grundregel lautet:
Substantiv + Adjektiv:
a **serious** *man*
Verb + Adverb:
He talks ***seriously****.*

Practice makes perfect

Use the word in brackets in the correct form to complete the sentences.

1. *No one takes me ____________________. (serious)*
2. *Steve is a _________________ man. (fascinating)*
3. *She's a ______________ person. (horrible)*
4. *He spoke ______________ to his wife. (horrible)*
5. *He looks after his money ___________. (careful)*

47. Money in or on the bank?

Wrong *I've got virtually no money on the bank.*
Right *I've got virtually no money **in** the bank.*

Erklärung

Geld liegt auf Englisch immer ‚**in** the bank' und ‚**in** your bank account'.
‚**in**' ist vor allem für geschlossene Räume oder Plätze richtig:

*The money is **in** my wallet.*
*My keys are **in** my pocket.*
*Geoff is **in** the next room.*

‚**on**' bedeutet meistens ‚on top of':

*The money is **on** top of the fridge.*
*There's a big bird **on** the roof.*
*Put the bowl **on** the table.*

Practice makes perfect

Finish the sentences using 'in' or 'on'.

1. *I think mum is ___ the kitchen.*
2. *When you've finished, put the milk back ___ the fridge.*
3. *The book you are looking for is ___ the kitchen table.*
4. *I always keep my credit card ___ my back pocket.*
5. *I saw Bob ___ the bank this morning.*

48. At or on Thursday?

Wrong *I'm going on holiday at Thursday.*
Right *I'm going on holiday* ***on*** *Thursday.*

Erklärung

‚on' benutzt man auch, wenn man von bestimmten Tagen spricht:
I always go swimming ***on*** *Mondays.*
There's a market in the square ***on*** *Saturdays.*
I always celebrate ***on*** *my birthday.*
I am visiting my grandmother ***on*** *Christmas Day.*
Roy came to see me ***on*** *Sunday afternoon.*
‚at' benutzt man für Zeiten:
I'm going to work ***at*** *eight.*

Practice makes perfect

Choose the correct word ('on/at') to finish the sentences.

1. *I hope it snows _____ Christmas.*
2. *I have to get up _____ five o'clock tomorrow.*
3. *Did you go to the party _____ New Year's Eve?*
4. *I bumped into Rob in town _____ Saturday afternoon.*
5. *We always try to go to church _____ Easter Sunday.*

49. On or at my face?

Wrong *I've got spots at my face.*
Right *I've got spots **on** my face.*

Erklärung

‚on' wird für die meisten Körperteile verwendet:
*She's got a tattoo **on** her arm.*
*He's got spots **on** his face.*
*He's got a big bruise **on** his leg.*
Für Mund, Auge und Ohr benutzt man **‚in'**:
*I've got something **in** my eye.*
*He's got an infection **in** his ear.*
*I've got an ulcer **in** my mouth.*

Practice makes perfect

Choose the correct word ('on/in') to finish the sentences.

1. *I think she was wearing a watch _____ her wrist.*
2. *The baby puts everything _____ his mouth.*
3. *Can you see any spots _____ my back?*
4. *She has a big hat _____ her head.*
5. *The music was so loud, I still have ringing _____ my ears.*

50. On or at the sofa?

Wrong *Let's sit at the sofa and cuddle.*
Right *Let's sit **on** the sofa and cuddle.*

Erklärung

Wenn man ‚obendrauf' sitzt oder liegt, wird **‚on'** verwendet:

*(to) sit **on** the chair*
*(to) sit **on** the stool*
*(to) sit **on** the sofa*
*I'm lying **on** the sofa because I'm tired.*

Aber aufpassen:

*You lie **in** bed.*
*You sit **at** the table/desk.*

Practice makes perfect

Choose the correct word ('on/at') to finish the sentences.

1. *Sit ____ the table and finish your meal!*
2. *I've been sitting ____ my desk all day.*
3. *Sit ____ the sofa and have a rest.*
4. *I don't like lying ____ bed all day.*
5. *Sit ____ the chair and have a cup of coffee.*

51. Get or have a baby?

Wrong *My sister is getting a baby in June.*
Right *My sister is **having** a baby in June.*

Erklärung

Achtung, falscher Freund! Manchmal werden im Englischen andere Vokabeln verwendet:

*You don't get a baby, you **have a baby**.*

Anderes Babyvokabular umfasst:

*My sister is **expecting**.*
*My wife is **pregnant**.*
*The baby is **due** in September.*
*We are awaiting **the patter of tiny feet** in August.*

Practice makes perfect

Use the correct word in the correct form to finish the sentences.

1. *Has Julia put on weight or is she ______________?*
2. *Sue got ______________ just after she got married.*
3. *The baby was ____________ last week, but nothing's happened yet.*
4. *We are ______________ our third child in June.*
5. *It won't be long now before we hear ________________________.*

52. Make or do homework?

Wrong *Did you make your homework last night?*
Right *Did you **do** your homework last night?*

Erklärung

Alles, was mit Arbeit zu tun hat, wird in Verbindung mit **‚(to) do'** beschrieben (auch zu Hause):

*I **do** some housework.*
*I **do** my homework.*
*I **did** some gardening.*

Nicht vergessen: **‚(to) make'** wird in der Regel für die Herstellung von etwas verwendet!

*I **made** a cake.*

Practice makes perfect

Use the correct form of the verbs 'make' or 'do' to complete these sentences.

1. *Yesterday I ______ my housework.*
2. *Paul is ______ a pizza. It smells good!*
3. *I ______ nothing at the weekend, I was too tired.*
4. *Paul ______ me a cup of tea when I arrived.*
5. *Are you ______ a cake?*

53. Real or really?

Wrong *It's a real big problem.*
Right *It's a **really** big problem.*

Erklärung

Adverbien werden nicht nur verwendet, um Verben zu beschreiben, sondern bei Adjektiven. Wenn man zum Beispiel das Wetter näher beschreiben will, könnte man sagen:

It's a hot day. – And how hot exactly? – It's a really hot day.

,very' und **,really'** sind die am häufigsten verwendeten Adverbien, aber es gibt anspruchsvollere:

*It expensive – it's **terribly** expensive.*
*It's cheap – it's **unbelievably** cheap.*
*You are beautiful – you are **incredibly** beautiful.*

Practice makes perfect

Describe the following things using an adverb and adjective, as in the example.

*A Rolls Royce – A Rolls Royce is **incredibly expensive**.*

1. *36 ° Celsius –* ______________________________
2. *A lazy day in bed –* ______________________________
3. *A bunch of red roses –* ______________________________
4. *A high-scoring football game –* ______________________________
5. *A cream cake –* ______________________________

54. Sudden or suddenly?

Wrong *The wall collapsed sudden.*
Right *The wall collapsed **suddenly**.*

Erklärung

Wenn man ein Verb näher beschreiben will, braucht man ein Adverb:

*The driver drove **quickly**.*
*The runner ran **slowly**.*
*The band played **loudly**.*
*Sue sang **nicely** at the party.*
*She cooks **badly**.*

Adverbien sind also immer mit irgendeiner Form von Aktion verbunden, irgendetwas muss passieren, jemand muss etwas tun. Beachte den Unterschied in folgenden Beispielen:

*Sue smells **well**. (Sie kann gut riechen, hat eine gute Nase.)*
*Sue smells **good**. (Sie riecht gut, trägt ein angenehmes Parfüm.)*

Practice makes perfect

Use the words in brackets in the correct form to complete the sentences.

1. *Paul is a __________ runner. (slow)*
2. *The police arrived _________. (quick)*
3. *She wore a _____________ dress last night. (beautiful)*
4. *It started to rain ____________. (sudden)*
5. *It wasn't an _________ decision to make. (easy)*

55. Condition or conditioning?

Wrong *Our hotel didn't have air condition.*
Right *Our hotel didn't have air* ***conditioning****.*

Erklärung

Eins von vielen Beispielen für falsch übersetzte Wörter! Andere Beispiele sind:

*congratulation**s**!*	– *NICHT: congratulation! (Immer den Plural benutzen!)*
*headquarter**s***	– *NICHT: headquarter (Immer den Plural benutzen!)*
*hair**dresser***	– *NICHT: haircutter*
*last order**s***	– *NICHT: last order*
*logistic**s***	– *NICHT: logistic*

Practice makes perfect

Choose the correct word from above to finish the sentences.

1. *My ____________ is pregnant, I'll have to find a new salon soon.*
2. *Get in touch with our __________ department to arrange delivery.*
3. *My company's ______________ are in the centre of town.*
4. *I believe ________________ are in order, you passed your exam!*
5. *It's freezing in here, please turn the __________________ off.*

56. At or on your birthday?

Wrong *I'll phone you at your birthday.*
Right *I'll phone you **on** your birthday.*

Erklärung

Verwende immer **,on'** für bestimmte Tage:
- ***on** Wednesday (Wochentage)*
- ***on** my mother's birthday (Geburtstage)*
- ***on** New Year's Day (besondere Tage im Jahr)*

Verwende **,at'** für Zeiten oder Zeiträume:
- ***at** three o'clock*
- ***at** lunchtime*
- ***at** Christmas*

Practice makes perfect

Choose the correct word ('at/on/in') to finish the sentences.

1. *I'll take you to lunch ___ your birthday.*
2. *I'll see you in the canteen ___ lunchtime.*
3. *In England we open our presents ___ Christmas Day.*
4. *I'm looking forward to a few days break ___ Easter.*
5. *Bob can't come ___ Sunday.*

57. Sleeping long?

Wrong *I like sleeping long at the weekend.*
Right *I like **having a lie-in** at the weekend.*

Erklärung

‚sleeping long' ist eine direkte Übersetzung! Andere Beispiele sind:

*He's sitting **on a bench**. (Sitzbank) – NICHT: bank (Geldinstitut)*
*He's writing **on the board.** (Tafel) – NICHT: table (Tisch)*
*The kids are **well-behaved**. (brav) – NICHT: brave (tapfer)*
*I'll buy **a packet of crisps**. (Chips) – NICHT: chips (Pommes)*
*What is your **opinion**? (Meinung) – NICHT: meaning (Bedeutung)*

Practice makes perfect

Use the examples above and the words in brackets to describe the situation.

The children are very quiet today. (well-behaved)
*The children **are well-behaved.***

1. *The teacher is writing an explanation down. (board)*

___

2. *Should I take the job or not? (opinion)*

___

3. *There are a lot of people in the park. (bench)*

___

4. *I can't pay for this all at once. (instalment)*

___

5. *I've been working like a dog. (lie-in)*

___

58. Live or living?

Wrong *I am living in London.*
Right *I **live** in London.*

Erklärung

‚simple present' oder ‚present progressive'? Für Dinge, die man immer tut, also für Gewohnheiten, benutzt man ‚**simple present**':

*I **work** in London.*

*Harry **plays** football every Thursday.*

Wenn man sagt: ‚I am **working** in London', bedeutet das, dass man nur eine befristete Stelle oder Aufgabe dort hat. Das **‚present progressive'** wird also für vorübergehende Situationen verwendet. Für Dinge, die jetzt, in diesem Moment passieren, oder für fortwährende Umstände:

***I'm reading** a good book at the moment.*

***They are building** a new road next to my office.*

Practice makes perfect

Decide if the sentences are right or wrong.	Right	Wrong
1. *I'm living with Jim, but I'm looking for my own flat.*	______	______
2. *I'm playing the guitar quite well.*	______	______
3. *I read a good book at the moment.*	______	______
4. *I'm looking for a new job.*	______	______
5. *My parents live in London, they love it there.*	______	______

59. Will or not?

Wrong *Tomorrow I will meet my brother in town.*
Right *Tomorrow I **am meeting** my brother in town.*

Erklärung

Das **‚will future'** kann nicht für feste Pläne in der Zukunft benutzt werden. Hierfür benötigt man die **ing-Form** des betreffenden Verbs mit einer Zeitangabe in der Zukunft:

*I **am meeting** Ray in the pub **tonight**.*
*I **am going** to Spain **in May**.*
*I **am meeting** Helen for a drink **this Friday**.*

Practice makes perfect

Write sentences about your future fixed plans.

1. *Tonight* ______________________________
2. *Tomorrow morning* ______________________________
3. *Summer holiday* ______________________________
4. *At the weekend* ______________________________
5. *Next bank holiday* ______________________________

60. Have or not?

Wrong *I have visited my mother yesterday.*
Right *I **visited** my mother yesterday.*

Erklärung

Im Englischen darf man die Zeiten nie durcheinanderbringen! Eine der Regeln für das **‚present perfect'** (‚I have …') lautet, dass es ohne feste Zeitangabe in der Vergangenheit verwendet wird:

*I **have done** my homework. (ohne Zeitangabe)*
*I **have written** a letter. (ohne Zeitangabe)*
*Kelly **has been** to Spain (irgendwann in der Vergangenheit)*

Practice makes perfect

Write sentences about yourself using 'I have' or 'I have never'.

1. *been to Spain?* ______________________________
2. *ridden a horse?* ______________________________
3. *learned French?* ______________________________
4. *tried sushi?* ______________________________
5. *bungee jumped?* ______________________________

61. Waited or waiting?

Wrong *When I saw Sally she waited for a bus.*
Right *When I saw Sally **she was waiting** for a bus.*

Erklärung

Die **ing-Form** des Verbs beschreibt vorübergehende Situationen von gewisser Dauer. Dies gilt für die Gegenwart (‚I **am doing** something now') und auch für die Vergangenheit:

*At eight o'clock **last night I was watching** the film. (past progressive)*
***Yesterday** I saw Paul, he **was waiting** at the bus stop. (past progressive)*

Practice makes perfect

Describe what you were doing in the following situations:

1. *This morning at six* ______________________________
2. *This time last year* ______________________________
3. *Last night at 10* ______________________________
4. *This time last week* ______________________________
5. *Last Saturday at 10 a.m.* ______________________________

62. Become or get?

Wrong *I became a new watch for my birthday.*
Right *I **got** a new watch for my birthday.*

Erklärung

Übersetzt man **‚(to) become'** ins Deutsche, heißt es **‚werden'**:
After 10 hours on the trail the walkers became tired.
I'm becoming sick and tired of his behavior.
Das deutsche **‚bekommen'** übersetzt man mit **‚(to) get'**:
My children always get too many presents at Christmas.
I get 30 days holiday a year.

Practice makes perfect

Use 'get' or 'become' in the correct form to finish the sentences.

1. *Did you ________ the report from Alan?*
2. *Who _______ custody of the children?*
3. *It _________ obvious to everyone that he didn't have a clue.*
4. *It is hard to _______ good staff these days.*
5. *Rob applied for the job, but he didn't _____ it.*

63. Introduce or introduction?

Wrong *Let me introduction you to my sister.*
Right *Let me* ***introduce*** *you to my sister.*

Erklärung

Achte darauf, Verben und Substantive nicht durcheinanderzubringen!
Das Verb beschreibt die Aktion:
We ***build*** *houses.*
Das Substantiv benennt einen Gegenstand oder eine Sache:
We are investing lots of money in ***buildings****.*

Practice makes perfect

Complete the chart.

Noun	Verb
publishing	
	(to) manufacture
fascination	
fantasy	
	(to) print
	(to) produce
	(to) involve

64. Catched or caught?

Wrong *I catched the ball and threw it back to Elsa.*
Right *I **caught** the ball and threw it back to Elsa.*

Erklärung

Im Englischen gibt es sehr viele unregelmäßige Verben, die in der einfachen Vergangenheitsform (**‚simple past'**) kein ‚ed' am Ende haben!

catch – ***caught*** – *NICHT: catched*
seek – ***sought*** – *NICHT: seeked*
ride – ***rode*** – *NICHT: rided*
hide – ***hid*** – *NICHT: hided*

Practice makes perfect

Turn the sentences into the simple past, using the correct form of the irregular verbs.

Simple present	Simple past
1. *I drive my car to work.*	____________________
2. *I drink a lot of beer.*	____________________
3. *I write 20 e-mails a day.*	____________________
4. *I find her behaviour strange.*	____________________
5. *I have a lot of backache.*	____________________

65. Make, do or have a party?

Wrong *Are you making a party on your birthday?*
Right *Are you **having** a party on your birthday?*

Erklärung

‚**(to) make**' wird oft falsch benutzt, denn es bedeutet auf Englisch lediglich so viel wie ‚etwas herstellen':

*You **make** a cake/a video/a chair.*

Außerdem gibt es die Redewendung:

(to) make fun of someone *(sich über jemanden lustig machen)*

In allen anderen Fällen werden auf Englisch andere Worte benutzt:

*You **have** a party. (Party machen)*
*You **do** your job. (seine Arbeit machen)*
It's fun. (etwas macht Spaß)
*We **had** so much fun. (etwas hat Spaß gemacht)*

Practice makes perfect

Choose the correct word ('make/do/have') in the correct form to finish the sentences.

1. *Are you still __________ a Spanish course?*
2. *Are you ___________ fun of me?*
3. *We _______ a lot of fun in the swimming pool.*
4. *Come with us to the show, _________ fun.*
5. *She only ________ the absolute minimum.*

66. Good weather or a good weather?

Wrong *Did you have a good weather on your holiday?*
Right *Did you have **good weather** on your holiday?*

Erklärung

Nicht vergessen: Unzählbare Substantive brauchen keine unbestimmten Artikel (‚a/an')!

*It's good **weather**.*
*It's **progress**.*
*It's too much **information**.*
*You get homework from your **teacher**.*

Practice makes perfect

Choose the correct word to finish the sentences.

*Have you lost **weight**/~~a weight~~?*

1. *Do you need advice/an advice?*
2. *Do you have news/a news about your brother?*
3. *We have an old furniture/old furniture in the cellar.*
4. *He can't breathe properly, he needs an oxygen/oxygen.*
5. *I don't need money/a money.*

67. Recipe or prescription?

Wrong *I got a recipe from the doctor.*
Right *I got a **prescription** from the doctor.*

Erklärung

Und schon wieder ein ‚false friend', auf den man achten sollte! Beim Arzt in England bekommt man eine **‚prescription'** ausgestellt, in Deutschland ein Rezept. Das Englische Wort **‚recipe'** ist auf Deutsch ein Kochrezept. Andere Beispiele:
Auf Deutsch kann man sich auf einem bestimmten Programm ein Programm anschauen. Auf Englisch wird ein **‚TV programme'** (Sendung) auf einem **‚TV channel'** (Sender, z. B. BBC 1) gezeigt.
Der englische ‚floor' ist nicht der ‚Flur', sondern der ‚Fußboden'! Also:

*The cat is on the **floor**. – The drinks machine is in the **corridor**.*

Und ‚(to) prove' heißt niemals ‚prüfen', sondern ‚beweisen'! Also:

*I **check** the engine to make sure it works. – I **prove** to the insurance company that someone fumbled with the breaks.*

Practice makes perfect

Choose the correct words from the brackets to finish the sentences.

1. *They put the photocopier in the ____________ outside my office. (floor/corridor)*
2. *Do you have a good _______________ for onion soup? (recipe/prescription)*
3. *Sat I is one of several German TV _______________. (programmes/channels)*
4. *The garage said they ____________ the oil but I couldn't _________ it. (checked/prove)*
5. *The doctor gave me a ______________ for painkillers. (recipe/prescription)*

68. Lend or borrow?

Wrong *Can you borrow me €50 until Friday?*
Right *Can you **lend** me €50 until Friday?*

Erklärung

Geld (oder etwas anderes) **an** jemanden verleihen heißt immer:
***(to) lend** money **to** someone*
Sich Geld (oder etwas anderes) **von** einer Bank (oder jemandem) leihen heißt immer:
***(to) borrow** money **from** someone/from a bank*

Practice makes perfect

Use 'lend' or 'borrow' in the correct form to finish the sentences.

1. *He's always ____________ money from his family and friends.*
2. *The bank wouldn't _______ me the money to buy a new car.*
3. *Can you ______ me €100 until the end of the month.*
4. *I _____________ €50 from Paula, but I paid it back.*
5. *Don't ________ him any money, you'll never see it again.*

69. Say or tell me?

Wrong *Can you say me the time?*
Right *Can you* ***tell*** *me the time?*

Erklärung

‚you **say something**' (sagen), aber ‚you **tell someone something**' (erzählen). Nach **‚(to) tell'** folgt meistens die Person, an die das Gesagte gerichtet ist. **‚(to) say'** wird in der Regel ohne Person benutzt:

Tom ***told*** *me he was ill.*
Tom ***said*** *he was ill.*

Practice makes perfect

Use 'say' or 'tell' in the correct form to finish the sentences.

1. *He ______ everyone to go.*
2. *Pete ______ me you lost your job?*
3. *Did she ______ goodbye to you?*
4. *Don't ______ me, let me guess!*
5. *What did your mum ______ when you ______ her?*

70. Bring or take?

Wrong *Paul is bringing us to the airport next week.*
Right *Paul is **taking** us to the airport next week.*

Erklärung

Bei der Entscheidung zwischen **‚bring'** oder **‚take'**, kommt es auf die (gedachte) Richtung der Handlung an!
‚Take me to …!' – zu einem Ort, an dem ich jetzt nicht bin.
‚Bring me back!' – hierher zurück an diesen Ort!
*Can you **take** this plate to the kitchen and **bring** me a cup of coffee.*
*Can you **take** me to work tomorrow?*

Practice makes perfect

Decide if these sentences are right or wrong, as in the example.

I took John to the airport last night. Right

1. *He took me to the cinema in his new car.* ________
2. *Stan brought me to the airport on Wednesday.* ________
3. *Can you bring me some bread from the bakery?* ________
4. *He is taking his grandma on holiday with him?* ________
5. *Has John taken the books with him?* ________

71. Lose or loose?

Wrong *Did you loose the game?*
Right *Did you **lose** the game?*

Erklärung

‚(to) lose' ist das Verb: verlieren (Achtung unregelmäßig: ‚lose – lost – lost').
‚loose' ist das Adjektiv: locker, nicht fest verpackt, nicht (mehr) eingesperrt:

*We **lost** the game 0-6.*
*This belt is very **loose**.*
*There's a tiger **loose** in the city!*

Practice makes perfect

Choose the correct word ('lose/loose') to finish the sentences.

1. *All the lions were roaming ________ on the prairie.*
2. *Did you win or ________?*
3. *He always has a lot of ________ change in his coat pockets.*
4. *The buckles on my shoes are ________.*
5. *In some countries it's important not to ______ face.*

72. Stop or stop with?

Wrong *Bob is trying to stop with smoking.*
Right *Bob is trying to stop **smoking**.*

Erklärung

Achtung, falscher Freund! ‚**mit** dem Rauchen aufhören' heißt auf Englisch einfach nur ‚**stop smoking**'!
Und um aus Verben Substantive zu machen (Gerundium), benutzt man auf Englisch die **ing-Form**:

*I hate **fighting**.*
*I love **shopping**.*
*We like **dancing**.*

Practice makes perfect

Finish the following sentences about things you do.

1. *I love* __________________________________.
2. *I hate* __________________________________.
3. *I don't like* ______________________________.
4. *I don't mind* _____________________________.
5. *I am trying to stop* ________________________.

73. Clear up or clean up?

Wrong *It took the police 12 hours to clean up after the accident.*
Right *It took the police 12 hours **to clear up** after the accident.*

Erklärung

‚**(to) clean up**' wird verwendet, wenn Dinge schmutzig sind und geputzt werden sollen:

*It's about time you **cleaned up** in your kitchen, it's filthy!*
*Are you going to **clean up** that mess you left in the bathroom?*

‚**(to) clear up**' dagegen heißt ‚aufräumen', das ist etwas anderes:

*Jenny, go and **clear up** your bedroom.*
*You'd better **clear up** those toys off the floor.*

Und hier noch eine Extravokabel: **‚(to) clear out'** heißt auch ‚Platz machen'.

*I **cleared out** the garage. We can get the car in there now.*

Practice makes perfect

Choose the correct expression to finish the sentences, as in the example.

*We ~~cleaned up~~/**cleared out** the garage to make way for our new car.*

1. *Yes, you can use my new mixer, but make sure you clean up/clear out afterwards.*
2. *Why don't you clean up/clear up all that mess in your wardrobe?*
3. *I cleaned out/cleared out all the old junk in the shed and sold it at the flea market.*
4. *He went to Vegas and cleaned up/cleared up.*
5. *I had to clear up/clear out after the kids again.*

74. It gives or there is?

Wrong *It gives a choice of three canteens at our plant.*
Right ***There is** a choice of three canteens at our plant.*

Erklärung

‚it gives‘ ist eine direkte Übersetzung aus dem Deutschen (‚es gibt‘), die es auf Englisch nicht gibt! Dort sagt man entweder **‚there is‘** oder **‚there are‘**:

***There are** five hotels in the town centre.*
***There is** a huge shopping mall on the edge of town.*

Practice makes perfect

Describe the place where you live using 'there is/there are' and the words in brackets.

1. *(parks)* ______________________________
2. *(hotels)* ______________________________
3. *(hospital)* ______________________________
4. *(golf course)* ______________________________
5. *(town hall)* ______________________________

75. On or in its place?

Wrong *Jill's flat is very tidy, everything is on its place.*
Right *Jill's flat is very tidy, everything is **in its place**.*

Erklärung

Sachen sind in der Regel **‚in a place'** oder **‚in their place'**, wenn sie an ihrem Ort sind:

*The dog's **in** its place in the kitchen.*
*Everything is **in** place.*

Menschen sind auf Englisch wie auf Deutsch z. B. ‚in einem Zimmer' oder ‚in einem Land':

*David came back from school. He's **in** his room now.*
*Where's Philip? **In** China!*

Practice makes perfect

Decide if these sentences are right or wrong, as in the example.

Eric's on the garage. Wrong – **in**

1. *Put the dirty laundry on the kitchen.* ______________
2. *That vase is on the wrong place!* ______________
3. *Where's mum? I think she's on the garden.* ______________
4. *Please put the glass back in the cupboard.* ______________
5. *I've hidden the money on a place no one will ever find.* ______________

76. Hard or hardly?

Wrong *Steve works hardly.*
Right *Steve works **hard**./Steve **hardly** works.*

Erklärung

‚**hard**' und ‚**hardly**' sind leicht zu verwechseln! ‚**hard**' ist sowohl ein Adjektiv als auch ein Adverb:

*John is a **hard** worker.*
*John works **hard**.*

‚**hardly**' ist ein anderes Wort und heißt ‚fast nie/fast nicht/kaum/selten':

*Mum **hardly** ever goes out nowadays.*
*Please speak up, I can **hardly** hear you.*

Practice makes perfect

Choose the correct word ('hard/hardly') to finish the sentences.

1. *It is really __________ to get a university place nowadays.*
2. *Betty is working __________ for her exams.*
3. *He puts __________ any effort into his job.*
4. *It is __________ my fault!*
5. *I __________ see Bob since he started his new job.*

77. Desert or dessert?

Wrong *Mum made a great desert yesterday.*
Right *Mum made a great* ***dessert*** *yesterday.*

Erklärung

Diese beiden Wörter werden oft nicht nur falsch benutzt, sondern auch falsch ausgesprochen!
‚a desert' ist eine Wüste. (Die Betonung liegt auf der **ersten** Silbe: ‚**des**-ert'; das ‚s' ist weich.)
‚a dessert' ist ein Nachtisch. (Die Betonung liegt auf der **zweiten** Silbe und das zweite ‚e' wird wie das englische 'hurt' gesprochen: ‚dis-**urt**'; das ‚s' ist ebenfalls weich.)

Practice makes perfect

Choose the correct word to finish the sentences.

*How many ~~desserts~~/**deserts** have you visited?*

1. *They were lost in the dessert/desert for days.*
2. *Rod's got a sweet tooth, he loves desserts/deserts.*
3. *Is the Gobi the biggest dessert/desert in the world?*
4. *What's for dessert/desert?*
5. *€35 Does that include dessert/desert?*

78. Sensible or sensitive?

Wrong *Be careful what you say to him, he's very sensible.*
Right *Be careful what you say to him, he's very* ***sensitive****.*

Erklärung

‚sensible' und ‚sensitive' verursachen ständig Probleme, da **‚sensible'** – dem deutschen ‚sensibel' so ähnlich – tatsächlich auf Deutsch ‚vernünftig' bedeutet:

Paul saves a lot of his money, he's very ***sensible****. (vernünftig)*
Roy is easily upset, he's very ***sensitive****. (empfindlich, sensibel)*

Practice makes perfect

Choose the correct word ('sensible/sensitive') to finish the sentences.

1. *It is a very ________________ situation.*
2. *Be ________________!*
3. *Negotiations are at a very ________________ stage.*
4. *He's party to a lot of ________________ information.*
5. *She works hard at school, she's a very ________________ girl.*

79. Personal or personnel?

Wrong *We have to reduce the number of personal.*
Right *We have to reduce the number of* ***personnel****.*

Erklärung

‚personal' wird verwendet, wenn wir über das Privatleben sprechen (Adjektiv: persönlich).
‚personnel' sind die Menschen, die für ein Unternehmen arbeiten (Substantiv: Personal).
Hier muss man mit der Rechtschreibung und mit der Aussprache aufpassen! ‚personnel' wird auf der dritten Silbe betont (‚person-**nel**'), ‚personal' auf der ersten (‚**per**-sonal').

Practice makes perfect

Choose the correct word ('personal/personnel') to finish the sentences.

1. ________________ *costs have sky-rocketed over the past year.*
2. *There is no need to get* ________________.
3. *We aren't taking on any* ________________ *at the moment.*
4. *I think she's got a lot of* ________________ *problems.*
5. *He always takes everything you say* ________________*ly.*

80. Don't or won't?

Wrong *He don't will be the boss much longer.*
Right *He **won't** be the boss much longer.*

Erklärung

Die negative Form von ‚will' ist **‚will not'**, die Kurzform ist **‚won't'** (sie wird im Englischen häufig verwendet).

Practice makes perfect

Describe the situation using 'will' or 'won't', as in the example.

Donald isn't interested in dancing.
*'He **won't** be going to the ball on Friday.'*

1. *Helen's company is closing down.*

   ____

2. *Harry knows nothing about computers.*

   ____

3. *Tim will be here in 10 minutes.*

   ____

4. *Sue is arriving 10 minutes after you leave.*

   ____

5. *You've smashed mum's new plate!*

   ____

81. Date or appointment?

Wrong *I have a date with my dentist.*
Right *I have an **appointment** with my dentist.*

Erklärung

Es ist wichtig, diese Worte nicht zu verwechseln!
‚an appointment' ist ein Termin zur Behandlung (beim Arzt) oder ein offizieller oder beruflicher Termin (Vorstellungsgespräch).
‚a date' ist eine persönliche Verabredung (zum Essen, ins Kino etc.).

Practice makes perfect

Decide if the following things are 'a date' or 'an appointment'.

1. *Your doctor is going to check your health.* ______________
2. *You are meeting someone for an intimate dinner.* ______________
3. *You have a job interview.* ______________
4. *You are having your eyes checked.* ______________
5. *You are meeting your new boyfriend/girlfriend.* ______________

82. Past or passed?

Wrong *I past my driving test.*
Right *I **passed** my driving test.*

Erklärung

‚past' ist ein Substantiv und bezeichnet die Vergangenheit:
*In the **past** I used to play a lot of volleyball.*
Es kann auch ein Adverb sein, wie in dem Ausdruck **‚(to) go past …'**:
*The procession went **past** my house.*
‚passed' hingegen ist die Vergangenheitsform des Verbs ‚(to) pass' und bedeutet, dass man eine Prüfung oder einen Test erfolgreich bestanden hat:
*I **passed** my driving test.*
Es kann außerdem bedeuten, dass etwas beendet oder vorüber ist:
*The storm has **passed**.*

Practice makes perfect

Describe the following situations using the word 'past' or 'passed', as in the example.

The wind has dropped and it has stopped raining. — *The storm **has passed**.*

1. *I used to live in Germany.* ______________________
2. *Joe's got his driving license!* ______________________
3. *I watched the demonstration from my bedroom window.* ______________________
4. *The optician said my eyes are fine.* ______________________
5. *My mum has stopped screaming.* ______________________

83. Play or playing?

Wrong *My brother is playing the guitar very well.*
Right *My brother **plays** the guitar very well.*

Erklärung

‚My brother **plays** the guitar' beschreibt eine Tatsache. ‚My brother **is playing** the guitar' beschreibt, was er jetzt gerade macht.
Die einfache Gegenwartsform **‚simple past'** wird für allgemeingültige Feststellungen gebraucht:

*He **plays** football.*
*She **cooks** really well.*

Die **ing-Form** des Verbs wird verwendet, wenn die aktuelle, jetzt gerade andauernde Situation beschrieben wird:

*Bob's not here, **he's playing** football.*
*Mum**'s cooking** dinner.*

Practice makes perfect

Describe the sentences on the left, as in the examples.

Bob's wearing pyjamas and lying in bed.	*Bob **is sleeping**.*
Bob does not stay up late.	*Bob **goes to sleep** very early.*
1. *Mum's in the kitchen, wearing an apron.*	______________________
2. *Mum always makes tasty things.*	______________________
3. *Dad's in the garage, under the car.*	______________________
4. *Kath is a superb piano player.*	______________________
5. *Kath is downstairs at the piano.*	______________________

84. Control or check?

Wrong *Our passports were controlled at the border.*
Right *Our passports were **checked** at the border.*

Erklärung

‚(to) control' heißt ‚etwas steuern' oder ‚leiten':
*He **controlled** the vehicle extremely well.*
*Sally knows how to **control** the school kids.*
‚(to) check' heißt ‚sich etwas genau ansehen' oder ‚prüfen':
*Have you **checked** the oil on the car?*
*Have you **checked** our bank balance recently?*

Practice makes perfect

Write a response to the statements on the left, using 'control' or 'check', as in the example.

Why did you crash?	*I lost **control** of the car.*
1. *Do you think the car has an oil leak?*	________________
2. *What did you think of the referee?*	________________
3. *Look at those kids running around wildly!*	________________
4. *She really likes to play being the boss!*	________________
5. *My passport has expired.*	________________

85. Briefly or shortly?

Wrong *My boss spoke shortly about the company's future plans.*
Right *My boss spoke **briefly** about the company's future plans.*

Erklärung

‚shortly' bedeutet ‚bald'. Deutsche verwechseln es gerne mit ‚briefly', aber nur **‚briefly'** bedeutet ‚kurz' und ‚für einen kurzen Zeitraum':

*My parents will be here **shortly**.*
*We spoke **briefly** about our holiday plans.*

Practice makes perfect

Choose the correct word ('shortly/briefly') to finish the sentences.

1. *I'm going to Portugal on holiday ________.*
2. *I lived in North America ________ when I was child.*
3. *It will ___________ be time to turn on the Christmas lights.*
4. *We went out together __________ when we were teenagers.*
5. *Harry is due to retire ________.*

86. Stationary or stationery?

Wrong *My wife drove into the back of a stationery lorry.*
Right *My wife drove into the back of a **stationary** lorry.*

Erklärung

Hier muss man ganz genau hinschauen!
‚stationary‘ (mit ‚a‘) bedeutet ‚stationär‘, ‚nicht in Bewegung‘.
‚stationery‘ (mit ‚e‘) beschreibt Büromaterial, z. B. Papier, Stifte oder Büroklammern:

*The car was **stationary** when it got hit by a bus*
*Did you order more office **stationery**?*

Practice makes perfect

Choose the correct word ('stationary/stationery') to finish the sentences.

1. *There's a shop that sells ________________ at the end of High Street.*
2. *Put the delivery of ________________ in the cupboard.*
3. ________________ *vehicles littered the motorway after the heavy snowstorm.*
4. *The ________________ lorry was loaded with ________________.*
5. *Our ________________ costs are ridiculous.*

87. True or the truth?

Wrong *Some people never speak the true.*
Right *Some people never speak the **truth**.*

Erklärung

‚**true**' ist ein Adjektiv und beschreibt als solches ein Substantiv genauer:
*The rumour is **true**.*
*It is **true** love.*
‚**truth**' ist das Substantiv und bedeutet ‚Wahrheit':
*It is the **truth**.*

Practice makes perfect

Decide if the following sentences are right or wrong, as in the example.

I didn't steal the money, and that's the true. Wrong – *That is the **truth**.*

1. *True love never runs smoothly.* ____________________
2. *Is it true that you are moving to Canada?* ____________________
3. *Paul insisted that it was a truth story.* ____________________
4. *I promise to tell the whole truth.* ____________________
5. *During the interrogation they gave him a true drug.* ____________________

88. Take off or put off?

Wrong *Put off your coat and make yourself comfortable.*
Right ***Take off*** *your coat and make yourself comfortable.*

Erklärung

‚**(to) take off**' in Verbindung mit Kleidung heißt ‚ablegen/ausziehen', bei Flugzeugen ‚abheben':

__Take off__ your shoes and sit down.
'We are __taking off__ in 30 minutes.

Beachte dabei: Auf Deutsch zieht man Kleidung an und wieder aus. Auf Englisch nicht!

You __put on__ your clothes and you __take off__ your clothes!
NICHT: put off your clothes!

‚**(to) put off**' bedeutet ‚etwas verzögern' oder auch ‚jmd. abschrecken' bzw. ‚abgeschreckt werden':

We've __put off__ the meeting until next week.
The restaurant was so dirty it __put__ me __off__ my food.

Practice makes perfect

Finish the sentences using 'take off' and 'put off' in the right context, as in the example.

I hate flying, especially __taking off__.

1. *I always ____________ doing my tax return until the last minute.*
2. *They've ____________ the budget meeting until the end of the month.*
3. *____________ your scarf, you must be boiling!*
4. *The plane ____________ on time.*
5. *Could you ____________ your shoes, I've just mopped the floor?*

89. High or height?

Wrong *The cupboard has a high of two metres.*
Right *The cupboard has **a height** of two metres.*

Erklärung

Abmessungen zu beschreiben, kann manchmal problematisch sein! Vor allem, wenn z. B. ‚high' und ‚Höhe' so ähnlich klingen. Aber man muss immer zwischen Adjektiv und Substantiv unterscheiden:

*two metres **high***	*– **a height** of two metres*
*two miles **wide***	*– **a width** of two miles*
*20 metres **long***	*– **a length** of 20 metres*
*It **weighs** 200 kilos.*	*– It has **a weight** of 200 kilos.*
*The water is 35 metres **deep**.*	*– It has **a depth** of 35 metres.*

Practice makes perfect

Use the words above to complete the sentences, as in the example.

*How **long** is the Channel Tunnel?*
*What is the **length** of the Channel Tunnel?*

1. *The bridge was nearly four kilometres ________.*
2. *What is the ________ of the water?*
3. *I'm not going on the diving board, it's too ________.*
4. *How much do you ________?*
5. *Did you measure the ________ of the garage?*

90. Your or you're?

Wrong *Your getting on my nerves.*
Right ***You're** getting on my nerves.*

Erklärung

Der Unterschied zwischen **‚your'** and **‚you're'** kann nur gesehen, nicht gehört werden! Es ist aber wichtig, dass man beide richtig schreibt und benutzt:
‚your' ist ein Possessivpronomen und wird für Eigentum oder Verwandte verwendet:

your car
your home
your wife

‚you're' ist die Kurzform von **‚you are'**:

***You're** only 27? – **You are** only 27!*

Practice makes perfect

Finish the sentences using 'you're' or 'your'.

1. *______ getting on my nerves!*
2. *Is that ______ neighbour over there?*
3. *How are ______ kids?*
4. *That's ______ problem!*
5. *______ not going to believe this!*

91. Quite or quiet?

Wrong *There were quiet a lot of people at the concert.*
Right *There were **quite** a lot of people at the concert.*

Erklärung

Zwei Worte, die fast gleich aussehen und auch noch fast gleich klingen, aber etwas völlig anderes bedeuten!
‚quiet' bedeutet ‚still', ‚ruhig'. Beim Aussprechen hört man das ‚e' (etwa ‚kwaiet')!

*It's very **quiet** in here.*
*The children are **quiet** today.*

‚quite' bedeutet ‚ziemlich' und klingt ziemlich abgehackt (nämlich ungefähr ‚kwait').

*It's **quite** cheap.*

Practice makes perfect

Choose 'quiet' or 'quite' to finish the sentences.

1. *It's not _______ what I expected.*
2. *We have _______ a lot of work to do on the new house.*
3. *Stop moaning, be _______!*
4. *Sam's keeping _______ about her new boyfriend.*
5. *The kids were _______ well-behaved today.*

92. Homework or housework?

Wrong *I did my English housework last night.*
Right *I did my English* ***homework*** *last night.*

Erklärung

‚housework' macht man, um die Wohnung sauber und ordentlich zu halten (staubsaugen, staubwischen, Küche und Bad putzen etc.):

I usually do my ***housework*** *on Saturday mornings.*

‚homework' hingegen macht man für die Schule, die Universität usw.:

Have you done your English ***homework*** *yet?*

Practice makes perfect

Choose the correct word ('housework/homework') to finish the sentences.

1. *My Latin __________ is impossible.*
2. *Does your maths teacher give you much __________?*
3. *Dave hates doing __________, his flat is really dirty.*
4. *Val's doing her __________, she's wearing rubber gloves.*
5. *I hope he doesn't give us any __________, I'm away all weekend.*

93. Shade or shadow?

Wrong *It was so hot, we spent most of the time in the shadow.*
Right *It was so hot, we spent most of the time* ***in the shade****.*

Erklärung

Dieser Fehler wird häufig gemacht, denn die zwei englischen Begriffe ‚shade' und ‚shadow' haben nur eine deutsche Entsprechung: Schatten.
‚a shadow' ist das, was eine Person oder ein Gebäude auf irgendeine Fläche wirft (den Schatten, nämlich ein Abbild der Person oder des Gebäudes).
‚the shade' hingegen ist das, wohin man geht, um nicht mehr in der Sonne zu sein (in den Schatten).

He's so nervous, he's afraid of his own ***shadow****.*
It was so hot in Egypt, it was 35 degrees ***in the shade****!*

Practice makes perfect

Choose the correct word ('shade/shadow') in the correct form to finish the sentences.

1. *As the sun went down, the trees cast long _________ on the sand.*
2. *It was hot, but we were sitting in the _________ of the palm trees.*
3. *The wind was blowing hard and it looked like the _________ were dancing on the lawn.*
4. *I saw a ghostly _________ go past the window.*
5. *Get out of the sun! Come and sit in the _________.*

94. While or during?

Wrong *John fell asleep during watching the film.*
Right *John fell asleep **while** watching the film.*

Erklärung

Beide Wörter ‚while' und ‚during' heißen auf Deutsch ‚während', auf Englisch muss man unterscheiden! Die Regel ist: **‚during'** + Substantiv:

*I ate a whole bag of crisps **during** the film.*

‚while' + Verb:

*I ate a whole bag of crisps **while** I was watching the film.*

Practice makes perfect

Describe the situation, using 'during' or 'while', as in the example.

John was watching the film, the phone rang.
*John answered the phone **while** he was watching the film.*

1. *Phil is at university, he has a part-time job.*

   ____

2. *Jack did his homework and ate a sandwich.*

   ____

3. *Sally had a shower, she flooded the bathroom.*

   ____

4. *Alan watched the film, then fell asleep.*

   ____

5. *The dog ran around the room, it smashed a vase.*

   ____

95. Holiday?

Wrong *We are going in holiday soon.*
Right *We are going **on holiday** soon.*

Erklärung

Man kann nur auf Deutsch ‚in die Ferien' fahren, auf Englisch muss man es etwas anders machen:

*You can **go on holiday**.*
*You can **take a holiday**.*
*You can **spend your holiday** somewhere.*

Auf Englisch ebenfalls unmöglich ist es, Urlaub ‚zu machen': 'You do not make (a) holiday.'

Practice makes perfect

Decide if these sentences are right or wrong, as in the example.

We are taking a holiday in Russia this year. Right

1. *We are going on holiday in two weeks.* ________
2. *Where did you spent your holidays last year?* ________
3. *We like to take our holidays after the school holidays.* ________
4. *Did you go to holiday last year?* ________
5. *Where's Bob? Is he at holiday?* ________

96. Perfect or perfectly?

Wrong *He speaks perfectly French.*
Right *He speaks **perfect** French.*

Erklärung

Ein Adjektiv beschreibt ein Substantiv (erste Spalte). Ein Adverb beschreibt ein Verb (zweite Spalte):

*He speaks **perfect** French. – He speaks French **perfectly**.*
*She is a **beautiful** singer. – She sings **beautifully**.*
*He is a **careful** driver. – He drives **carefully**.*

Außerdem kann ein Adverb auch ein Adjektiv beschreiben:

*Her singing is **perfectly** beautiful.*

Practice makes perfect

Complete the table using an adjective or an adverb.

1. *Roy is a bad driver. – He drives* ___________.
2. *They are a good team. – They play* ___________.
3. *He is a* ___________ *cook. – He cooks wonderfully.*
4. *Steve is a hard worker. – Steve works* ___________.
5. *She is a terrible teacher. – She teaches* ___________.
6. *Colin is a quick runner. – Colin runs* ___________.

97. Remind or remember?

Wrong *Remember me to phone Alison about the job.*
Right **_Remind me_** *to phone Alison about the job.*

Erklärung

‚**(to) remind**' bedeutet ‚jmd. an etwas erinnern' (auf Deutsch und auf Englisch ein transitives Verb):

*Please **remind me** to pay the gas bill.*
*Did you **remind Joe** about mum's birthday?*

‚**(to) remember**' bedeutet ‚sich an etwas erinnern' (auf Deutsch ein reflexives Verb):

***I remember you!** We were in the same class at school?*
(Ich erinnere mich an dich.)
***Do you remember** our first holiday in Crete?*
(Ich erinnere mich an diesen Urlaub.)
***Remember** me!*
(Erinnere dich an mich, d. h. vergiss mich nicht!)

Practice makes perfect

Choose the right word to finish the sentences.

1. *Do you remind/remember me?*
2. *Did you remind/remember to switch off the light?*
3. *You always have to remind/remember her to pay her half.*
4. *He reminds/remembers me of someone.*
5. *That reminds/remembers me, you owe me €20!*

250 Fehler

98. Actual or current?

Wrong *I don't like my actual job.*
Right *I don't like my **current** job.*

Erklärung

Auch hier gibt es immer wieder Probleme, weil ein englisches Wort genauso klingt wie ein deutsches, aber etwas völlig anderes bedeutet! **‚actual'** heißt auf Deutsch ‚tatsächlich, wahr, echt, eigentlich'. Es bedeutet NICHT ‚aktuell':

*What is the **actual** state of the company's finances?*
*What is your **actual** opinion?*

Das deutsche ‚aktuell' (jetzt, zur Zeit) heißt auf Englisch **‚current'**, die adverbiale Form lautet **‚currently'**:

*What is the **current** position?*
*Where are you working **currently**?*

Practice makes perfect

Choose the correct word to finish the sentences.

1. *We don't know the actual/current situation, there is a lot of confusion.*
2. *What is your actual/current address?*
3. *I don't actually/currently know.*
4. *These are the actual/current clothes he wore in the film.*
5. *We are actually/currently considering our options.*

99. Clock or watch?

Wrong *Stop looking at your clock!*
Right *Stop looking at your **watch**!*

Erklärung

‚a watch' trägt man bei sich, die Armbanduhr am Handgelenk (‚wrist'), daher auch der Ausdruck ‚wristwatch', die Taschenuhr (‚pocket watch') in einer Uhrentasche der Weste oder Hose.
‚a clock' steht oder hängt! Diese Uhr wird niemals an der eigenen Person getragen.

*He kept looking at **the clock on the wall**.*
*She keeps looking at **her watch**!*

Practice makes perfect

Choose the correct word to finish the sentences.

1. *My alarm clock/watch always rings at six.*
2. *Have you got a stopwatch/stopclock which I can borrow?*
3. *The time won't go any quicker just because you keep looking at the clock/watch on the wall.*
4. *Ok, let's synchronise our clocks/watches.*
5. *My parents bought me a lovely bedside watch/clock for my birthday.*

100. Same than or same as?

Wrong *You are just the same than your brother.*
Right *You are just the* ***same as*** *your brother.*

Erklärung

‚as‘ vergleicht Dinge, die gleich sind:
This is the ***same as*** *the other stuff.*
This firm is ***as useless as*** *the other firm.*
‚than‘ zeigt an, dass es Unterschiede gibt:
You are ***bigger than*** *me.*
New York is ***much bigger than*** *Bonn.*

Practice makes perfect

Use the information below to write sentences about the two companies, using ‘as’ or ‘than’, as in the example.

	Smith & Son	Wilson & Co
1.	*250 employees*	*200 employees*
2.	*10 branches*	*15 branches*
3.	*2 warehouses*	*2 warehouses*
4.	*10,000 sq. metres office space*	*11,000 sq. metres office space*
5.	*€4 turnover*	*€2.5 turnover*
6.	*30 lorries*	*30 lorries*

1. *Smith & Son have more employees* ***than*** *Wilson & Co.*

2. ______________________________

3. ______________________________

4. ______________________________

5. ______________________________

6. ______________________________

101. How expensive?

Wrong *Your hotel is expensiver than ours.*
Right *Your hotel is **more expensive** than ours.*

Erklärung

Für die Steigerung von Adjektiven muss man sich drei Dinge merken!

1. Kurze Adjektive (eine Silbe) + ‚er':
   *small – small**er**, big – bigg**er**, long – long**er***
2. Längere Adjektive (zwei Silben oder mehr) mit ‚more':
   *afraid – **more** afraid, expensive – **more** expensive*
   *serious – **more** serious, exciting – **more** exciting*
3. Ausnahme: Adjektive auf ‚y':
   *sunny – sunn**ier**, lazy – laz**ier**, cosy – cos**ier***

Practice makes perfect

Compare the two department stores using the information below.

	Homestore	Hardy
1.	5 % discount for staff	10 % discount for staff
2.	9,000 square metres	10,000 square metres
3.	Rent: € 8000 per month	Rent: € 7000
4.	Range of 15000 products	Range of 16000 products
5.	New building	Old building
6.	Average age of staff: 28	Average age of staff: 36

*1. The Homestore staff discount is **lower than** the Hardy staff discount.*

2. ______________________________

3. ______________________________

4. ______________________________

5. ______________________________

6. ______________________________

102. In or on the radio/TV?

Wrong *Did you see the great film in TV last night?*
Right *Did you see the great film* ***on TV*** *last night?*

Erklärung

Präpositionen sind nicht einfach und sehr oft anders als im Deutschen!
Sendungen laufen **‚on TV'** oder **‚on the TV'**:

I sometimes watch sport ***on TV****.*

I never watch the news ***on the TV****.*

Was immer man hört, man hört es **‚on the radio'**:

I always listen to music ***on the radio****.*

On Saturday I listen to the football ***on the radio.***

Practice makes perfect

Write sentences using the words in brackets, as in the example.

(sport/TV) *I watch a lot of sport* ***on TV****.*

1. *(music/radio)* ______________________________
2. *(news/radio)* ______________________________
3. *(live sport/TV)* ______________________________
4. *(films/TV)* ______________________________
5. *(plays/radio)* ______________________________

103. Article or not?

Wrong *I'm technician at the power plant.*
Right *I'm **a technician** at the power plant.*

Erklärung

Zählbare Substantive im Singular können nicht ohne Artikel verwendet werden:

*I'm **a teacher** at a language school.*
*My daughter is **a vegetarian**.*
*Japanese is **a difficult language** to learn.*

Zählbare Substantive im Plural können ohne Artikel verwendet werden:

*We are **teachers** at a language school.*
*Japanese and French are difficult **languages** to learn.*

Practice makes perfect

Use the information on the left to write a sentence on the right, using an article if necessary, as in the example.

Rick works in school, his subject is French. *He's **a teacher**.*

1. *Bob and Phil drive taxis for a living.* ____________________
2. *My dad treats patients.* ____________________
3. *Sally and Jill have their own company.* ____________________
4. *Tim doesn't drink alcohol.* ____________________
5. *Sue and Fey have known each other all their lives.* ____________________

250 Fehler

104. Like play or playing?

Wrong *I like it to play table tennis.*
Right *I **like playing** table tennis.*

Erklärung

Verben wie ‚mögen', ‚lieben', ‚hassen', ‚bevorzugen' usw. werden in der Regel von einem Verb in der ***ing-Form*** gefolgt:

*I **like playing** badminton.*
*I **don't like working** at the weekend.*
*I **hate getting up** in the morning.*
*I **love travelling** to new places.*
*I **prefer eating meat** to fish.*
*I **don't mind helping** in the garden.*

Practice makes perfect

Use the preference verbs above and the words in brackets in the correct form to write about yourself, as in the example.

(sit/sun) — *I **don't like sitting** in the sun.*

1. *(eat/nice restaurants)* ____________________
2. *(read/good books)* ____________________
3. *(red wine/white wine)* ____________________
4. *(do/homework)* ____________________
5. *(play/card games)* ____________________

105. In or at school?

Wrong *My daughter doesn't work, she's in school.*
Right *My daughter doesn't work, she's* ***at school****.*

Erklärung

Den Ausdruck ‚in school' für ‚in der Schule' benutzt man auf Englisch nicht. Spricht man über die Ausbildung der Kinder, heißt es immer **‚at'**:

My daughter is ***at*** *school,* ***at*** *university,* ***at*** *college, etc.*
Does your son have a job? – No, he's ***at*** *university.*
Has your daughter started working yet? – No, she's still ***at*** *school.*

Auch wenn es um den jetzigen Aufenthaltsort geht, verwendet man **‚at'**:

Is your daughter at home? – No, she is ***at school*** *right now.*

Practice makes perfect

Describe what the following people do, as in the examples.

The youngest person you know *My sister is* ***at*** *school.*

1. *A 10-year-old girl* ______________________________
2. *Someone studying history* ______________________________
3. *A young man who wants to be a teacher* ______________________________
4. *A child who has just left nursery* ______________________________
5. *A girl who has just done her 'A' levels* ______________________________

106. Going home or going to home?

Wrong *I've had enough, I'm going to home.*
Right *I've had enough, I'm going **home**.*

Erklärung

‚at home' wird verwendet, um zu sagen, wo man gerade ist oder war, nämlich ‚zu Hause':

*Where are you? – I'm **at home**.*
*Did you go out last night? – No, I stayed **at home**.*

‚home' ohne Präposition verwendet man, um zu sagen, wohin man geht, nämlich ‚nach Hause':

*Where are you going? – I'm going **home**.*

Practice makes perfect

Answer the following questions, using 'home' in the correct context.

*Where do you keep your bicycle? – I keep it **at home.***

1. *What do you usually do when you finish work/school?* ________________
2. *What do most people do when the pubs shut?* ________________
3. *What do you say to your colleagues when you leave work/school?* ________________
4. *Where are you usually at 11 o'clock in the evening?* ________________
5. *What do people do at the end of a party?* ________________

107. S or not?

Wrong *You got the job? Congratulation!*
Right *You got the job? **Congratulations**!*

Erklärung

Ein Plural-s ist bei allen folgenden Ausdrücken zwingend nötig, entweder weil es im Englischen (anders als im Deutschen) einfach so ist (Sprachgebrauch) oder weil es die Logik erfordert:

__Congratulations__, you have won € 1000. (Sprachgebrauch)
Last __orders__, please! (Sprachgebrauch)
We can meet at our company's __headquarters__. (Sprachgebrauch)
One of my __friends__ is a doctor. (Logik!)
I have worked here for six __months__. (Logik!)

Practice makes perfect

Choose the correct word to finish the sentences.

1. *Paul is a good friend/friends of mine.*
2. *Can you wait for two minute/minutes, please?*
3. *I can't believe my little baby is already six month/months old!*
4. *Did he say 'congratulate'/'congratulations'?*
5. *He was one of the best teacher/teachers at our school.*

108. In or at an age?

Wrong *I got married in the age of 26.*
Right *I got married* ***at the age*** *of 26.*

Erklärung

Der deutsche Ausdruck ‚im Alter von 26 Jahren' wird oft als ‚in the age of 26' übersetzt. Das ist ein falscher Freund und nicht korrekt! Richtig heißt es:

at the age *of 26*

Die Kurzform **‚at 26'** kann ebenfalls verwendet werden. ‚with 26' ist leider auch völlig falsch.

Practice makes perfect

Answer the questions using 'at'.

1. *When did you/will you leave school?* ______________________
2. *When can you legally drink alcohol in your country?* ______________
3. *When are you eligible to vote in your country?* ________________
4. *When can you start taking driving lessons?* __________________
5. *When can you buy cigarettes in your country?* ________________

109. Married with or married to?

Wrong *Roy is married with a model.*
Right *Roy is* ***married to*** *a model.*

Erklärung

Auch hier gilt: Das wörtliche Übersetzen führt meistens zum falschen Ergebnis! **‚married'** wird auf Englisch mit **‚to'** verwendet, nie mit ‚with' (wie im Deutschen).

Practice makes perfect

Describe the following relationships, as in the example.

Phil's wife takes her clothes off for a living.
He's ***married to*** *a stripper.*

1. *Jill's husband is a man of the cloth.*

   ____

2. *Dave's wife works with figures.*

   ____

3. *Key's husband has a really dangerous job.*

   ____

4. *Alan's wife doesn't speak English.*

   ____

5. *Susie's partner delivers letters.*

   ____

110. On or at Christmas?

Wrong *Are you going away on Christmas?*
Right *Are you going away **at Christmas**?*

Erklärung

Spricht man über einen der großen Feiertage, an denen viele Menschen Urlaub machen, wird **‚at'** verwendet:

***at** Christmas*
***at** Easter*
***at** Whitsuntide (Pfingsten)*

Nicht vergessen:

***in** the morning, **in** the afternoon, **in** the evening, ABER: **at** night*
***in** the morning, ABER: **on** Friday morning*
***on** your birthday*
***on** Monday*
***on** 22nd June*

Practice makes perfect

Answer the following questions using 'at' or 'on', as in the example.

When do you get the most presents? ***On** my birthday.*

1. *When does a cat usually go out on the prowl?* ____________________
2. *When do you open your Christmas presents?* ____________________
3. *When do most people do their shopping?* ____________________
4. *When is your birthday?* ____________________
5. *When do you send cards to people?* ____________________

111. From or of?

Wrong *Have you got a photo from your new girlfriend?*
Right *Have you got a photo **of** your new girlfriend?*

Erklärung

Das deutsche ‚von' hat im Englischen zwei Entsprechungen, die oft verwechselt werden!
‚of' bezeichnet eine Zugehörigkeit und wird mit den folgenden Ausdrücken verwendet:

*a photo **of** someone: Sabine showed me a photo **of** her new baby. – Your mother showed me a picture **of** you when you were a baby.*
*the price **of** something: What's the price **of** a new computer? – Some people know the price **of** everything, but the value **of** nothing.*

‚from' bezeichnet einen Ausgangspunkt oder eine Herkunft und kann in folgenden Fällen eingesetzt werden:

*Our prices start **from** €300.*
*That photo is **from** 1998.*

Practice makes perfect

Look at the sentence on the left, then write about it on the right!

Helen had an album of photographs. *She showed us photos **of** her daughter.*

1. *Their cheapest car is €4000.* ____________________
2. *Is that you at school in that picture?* ____________________
3. *Was that taken in the 1980s?* ____________________
4. *How much are your shares worth now?* ____________________
5. *Is that your dad?* ____________________

112. Do you or would you?

Wrong *Do you like something to eat?*
Right ***Would you** like something to eat?*

Erklärung

‚do you like' ist die Hilfsverbkonstruktion, die man vor einem Vollverb benötigt, um danach zu fragen, ob jemand etwas generell mag:

***Do you like** sandwiches?*
***Do you like** coffee?*

‚would you like' entspricht dem deutschen ‚möchtest du' und wird verwendet, um zu fragen, ob jemand etwas Bestimmtes haben will:

*Are you hungry? **Would you like** something to eat?*
***Would you like** to sit down?*

Practice makes perfect

Ask questions to find out the information, as in the example.

Ask if someone is thirsty.	***Would you** like a drink?*
1. *Find out if someone likes tennis.*	______________________
2. *Find out if someone wants a game of tennis.*	______________________
3. *Ask if someone is hungry.*	______________________
4. *Find out if someone is feeling sick or not?*	______________________
5. *Find out if someone likes Pink Floyd.*	______________________

113. Careful or carefully?

Wrong *Be carefully!*
Right *Be **careful**!*

Erklärung

Ein Adverb (z. B. **‚carefully'**) beschreibt eine Aktion genauer:

*He drives **carefully**.*

*She trod very **slowly** along the steep path.*

Ein Adjektiv (z. B. **‚careful'**) wird immer mit dem Verb **‚to be'** verwendet – dabei kann es die Form einer Beschreibung oder auch eines Befehls annehmen:

***Be** quiet!*

***Don't be** stupid!*

***Be** good!*

*It could **be** dangerous.*

Practice makes perfect

Choose the correct word to finish the sentences, as in the example.

*Jack is always **careful**/~~carefully~~ when he's chopping wood.*

1. *Rick said he'd be quiet/quietly if he gets home late.*
2. *He answered all the questions truthful/truthfully.*
3. *Can't you be sensible/sensibly about this?*
4. *I tried to be fair/fairly, but it was impossible.*
5. *I didn't realize it would be so expensive/so expensively.*

114. Two weeks?

Wrong *We were two weeks in Spain.*
Right *We were in Spain **for two weeks**.*

Erklärung

Im Englischen folgt der Satzbau der Regel ‚Ort vor Zeit', zuerst wird also immer der Ort, dann die Zeit genannt:
*I lived **in London for two years**.*
(Ort: in London – Zeit: for two years)
*I went **to the cinema last night**.*
(Ort: to the cinema – Zeit: last night)

Practice makes perfect

Write sentences using the words in the brackets, as in the example.

*(swimming/last time) – The last time I went swimming was **in June**.*

1. *(as a child/lived/Manchester)*

___

2. *(best friend/saw)*

___

3 . *(a DVD/watch)*

___

4. *(last exam/in 1998)*

___

5. *(hot country/holiday/in 2011)*

___

115. A or an?

Wrong *Do you have a Internet connection in your bedroom?*
Right *Do you have* ***an*** *Internet connection in your bedroom?*

Erklärung

Vor einem Vokal (a, e, i, o, u) wird der unbestimmte Artikel ‚a' zu ‚**an**':
Do you want ***an*** *apple or a banana?*
Did you really sleep in ***an*** *igloo when you went to Lapland?*

Practice makes perfect

Use 'a' or 'an' to finish these sentences, as in the example.

I went swimming with dolphins, it was ***an*** *amazing experience.*

1. *Joe is ____ nice old man.*
2. *I bit into ____ juicy apple and broke one of my teeth!*
3. *Mum made me ____ egg and four pieces of toast for breakfast.*
4. *It was ____ horrible night, the storm was frightening.*
5. *It was ____ truly exciting experience.*

116. At or on a floor?

Wrong *My new office is at the 15th floor.*
Right *My new office is **on** the 15th floor.*

Erklärung

Spricht man über eine Etage oder ein Stockwerk, verwendet man die Präposition **‚on'**:

*Are you still **on** the ground floor?*
*We had to park the car **on** the top storey of the car park.*

Aber Achtung:

*My father has a large work room **in** the basement/**in** the cellar.*
*I found some old photos **in** the attic.*

Practice makes perfect

Describe where the following things can be found using 'on' or 'in'.

1. *Your office/classroom.* ______________________________
2. *Your heating system at home.* ______________________________
3. *Large quantities of wine.* ______________________________
4. *Old clothes and toys.* ______________________________
5. *An underground car park.* ______________________________

117. Interested on or in something?

Wrong *I'm not interested on politics.*
Right *I'm not interested **in** politics.*

Erklärung

Im Gegensatz zum Deutschen zeigt man auf Englisch nicht ‚an' etwas Interesse, sondern ist **‚in'** etwas interessiert oder nicht:

*He's interested **in** football.*
*She's interested **in** Ancient Greek.*

Wörtliches Übersetzen macht ‚interested on something' zu einem häufigen Fehler!

Practice makes perfect

Write sentences to describe the situation on the left, as in the example.

*Mary hates sport. Mary is **not interested in** sport.*

1. *Al is quite happy in his job.* ________________________________
2. *Jake loves reading.* ________________________________
3. *I don't like history.* ________________________________
4. *Sally enthuses about bungee-jumping.* ________________________________
5. *She doesn't seem to like me!* ________________________________

118. Italy or Italian?

Wrong *Can you speak Italy?*
Right *Can you speak **Italian**?*

Erklärung

Nationalitäten nicht mit den dazugehörigen Ländern verwechseln!

Germany – *German*
Switzerland – *Swiss*
Israel – *Israeli*
Holland – *Dutch*

Practice makes perfect

Complete the graph.

Country	Nationality	Sentences
Wales		*Rick's from Wales, I think.*
Malta		
	Burmese	
	Greek	*Would you like a Greek salad?*
Peru		
Belgium		
Nicaragua		
New Zealand		
	Croatian	
Cameroon		

119. Not or don't?

Wrong *I not like sushi.*
Right *I **don't like** sushi.*

Erklärung

Die meisten Verben (‚like', ‚have', ‚drive' etc.) werden im **‚simple present'** mit **‚do not'** verneint, das die Form **‚don't'** (oder **‚doesn't'**) annimmt. In der Regel sind dies allgemeine negative Einstellungen:

*He likes tennis. – I **don't like** tennis.*
*She watches a lot of reality TV, but he **doesn't** watch reality TV.*

Nur das Verb ‚to be' wird ohne ‚do' mit **‚not'** verneint, wenn man z. B. im **‚present progressive'** eine gerade andauernde Situation beschreibt:

I'm listening.
*I'm **not** listening.*

Diese Regel gilt auch, wenn ‚to be' in Verbindung mit Adjektiven steht:

*I'm hungry – I'm **not** hungry.*
*She's nice. – She's **not** nice.*

Practice makes perfect

Write sentences to describe the situation on the left, as in the example.

*Rod takes no interest at school. Rod **doesn't like** school.*

1. *Sue never concentrates.* ____________________
2. *Harry doesn't have a car.* ____________________
3. *Mum never flies.* ____________________
4. *Val is not listening to me.* ____________________
5. *Judy is off sick.* ____________________

120. The birthday?

Wrong *Tomorrow is the birthday of my father.*
Right *It's **my father's birthday** tomorrow.*

Erklärung

Die Zugehörigkeit einer Sache zu einer Person (Genitiv) wird durch Apostroph mit **‚s'** angezeigt:

*It's **my mum's** birthday. – NICHT: the birthday of my mum*
*That's **my brother's** car. – NICHT: the car of my brother*

Außerdem schleicht sich bei Geburtstagen gerne ein falscher Freund ein: Im Englischen ‚hat' man nicht Geburtstag, sondern ein Geburtstag ‚ist' oder ‚war':

*It **is** my birthday today.*
*It **was** my birthday yesterday.*

Practice makes perfect

Use the information on the left to write sentences, as in the example.

The car in the garage belongs to my brother.	*It's **my brother's car**.*
1. *Rob's birthday is on the 20th. It's the 20th today.*	______________________
2. *My birthday is on the 2nd, it was the 2nd yesterday.*	______________________
3. *The house on the corner belongs to Bill.*	______________________
4. *That little bike belongs to my daughter.*	______________________
5. *I think Rob owns that wallet.*	______________________

121. Work by or at?

Wrong *I work by the post office.*
Right *I work **at** the post office.*

Erklärung

Menschen arbeiten **‚at'** einer Firma oder **‚for'** jemanden (auf Deutsch beides ‚für'):

I work at ICU.

*I work **for** my brother.*

Jemand kann auch **‚with'** einer Firma arbeiten (auf Deutsch ‚bei'):

*I'm **with** Lloyd's Bank.*

*I'm **with** the railways.*

Auch möglich ist eine Arbeit ‚in' einem bestimmten Bereich:

*Joe's **in** advertising.*

‚by' allerdings ist eine wörtliche Übersetzung und in diesen Fällen immer falsch!

Practice makes perfect

Decide if the sentences are right or wrong, as in the example.

I work at my brother. Wrong – ***for***

1. *I'm by Bolger's.* __________

2. *I work for an engineering company.* __________

3. *Sheila's in marketing.* __________

4. *Betty's got a job at the new shopping mall.* __________

5. *I wouldn't like to work by him!* __________

122. For or since?

Wrong *I am married since 2008.*
Right *I **have been married** since 2008.*

Erklärung

Um diesen Satz korrekt zu bilden, muss man das **‚present perfect'** verwenden – die Zeitform, die vielleicht am schwierigsten zu verstehen und zu meistern ist, denn man kann sie auf so viele verschiedene Arten benutzen.
In diesem Fall beschreibt das **‚present perfect'**, wie lange etwas bis jetzt oder heute andauert:

how long … until now
*I **am married.***
(eine Tatsache)
*I **have been married since** 2008.*
(ein Zeitraum, seit 2008 bis heute)
*I **live** in Munich.*
(eine Tatsache)
*I **have lived** in Munich for 10 years.'*
(ein Zeitraum, seit 10 Jahren und immer noch)

Achtung: Eine andere Bedeutung hat dagegen die Verwendung des **‚simple past'**:

*I **lived** in Munich for 10 years.'*
(auch ein Zeitraum, aber 10 Jahre lang und jetzt nicht mehr!)

Practice makes perfect

Use the present perfect and 'for' or 'since' to answer the questions about yourself.

1. *How long have you lived in your current home?*

   ____

2. *How long have you been reading this book?*

   ____

3. *How long have you been going to work/school?*

   ____

4. *How long have you known your English teacher?*

   ____

5. *How long have you been learning English?*

   ____

123. Don't or doesn't?

Wrong *He don't speak English.*
Right *He **doesn't** speak English.*

Erklärung

Hier kommt alles zusammen: ein unregelmäßiges Verb, die dritte Person Singular (braucht ein ‚s') und eine Verneinung! Bei so vielen Besonderheiten verwundert es nicht, dass dieses kleine Wort so häufig falsch konstruiert wird.
Merke: ‚He don't' und ‚she don't' existieren nicht!

I don't/we don't/you don't/they don't

ABER:

*he/she/it **doesn't***
*He **doesn't** understand.*
*She **doesn't** like me.*
*It **doesn't** matter.*

Practice makes perfect

Use 'don't' or 'doesn't' to describe the sentences on the left, as in the example.

It's been raining all day. *'It **doesn't** look good for the barbecue tonight.'*

1. *He eats a lot of junk food.* ______________________
2. *They have poorly paid jobs.* ______________________
3. *The dog sleeps outside.* ______________________
4. *We spend all the money we earn.* ______________________
5. *She can't understand what I'm saying.* ______________________

124. Good or well-organized?

Wrong *The conference wasn't good organized.*
Right *The conference wasn't* ***well-organized****.*

Erklärung

Manchmal wird die dritte Form des Verbs (das Partizip/‚**past participle**') als Adjektiv verwendet, um ein Substantiv zu beschreiben. Wird dieses Partizip seinerseits ergänzt, dann um ein Adverb, was im Fall von ‚well' mit dem Partizip zu einem eigenen neuen Wort verschmilzt:

written – The book was ***well-written****. – NICHT: good written*
spoken – He was very ***well-spoken****. – NICHT: good spoken*

Keine Verschmelzung dann hier:

The conference was badly organized.

Practice makes perfect

Describe the following things using an adverb and the past participle, as in the example.

An efficient department *An efficient department is* ***well-run****.*

1. *An inefficient department* ____________________
2. *An intelligent woman* ____________________
3. *A top executive* ____________________
4. *An efficient worker* ____________________
5. *A good book* ____________________

125. React on or to?

Wrong *He reacted badly on the news.*
Right *He reacted badly* ***to*** *the news.*

Erklärung

Menschen reagieren auf Englisch immer ‚**to** something' (auf Dinge oder Situationen):

The government didn't react ***to*** *the crisis quickly enough.*
How did he react ***to*** *your criticism?*

Practice makes perfect

Write a sentence to describe the sentence on the right, as in the example.

The situation after the earthquake was a complete disaster.
The authorities reacted badly ***to*** *the emergency.*

1. *Christine started crying.* ______________________________
2. *He started throwing punches.* ______________________________
3. *He totally ignored the hecklers.* ______________________________
4. *He sent €50 to the charity.* ______________________________
5. *The government sent troops in.* ______________________________

126. Search or look for?

Wrong *I am searching for a new job.*
Right *I am **looking for** a new job.*

Erklärung

‚(to) search‘ und **‚a search‘** werden vor allem in offiziellen Zusammenhängen verwendet:

*Police are **searching for** the escaped convict.*
*He was **searched** at the airport.*
*They are carrying out a house to house **search**.*

Die alltäglichere Bedeutung von ‚suchen‘ wird von dem Verb **‚(to) look for‘** abgedeckt:

*I'm **looking for** my keys, have you seen them?*
*I'm **looking for** a new job, I can't stand my boss.*

Practice makes perfect

Use 'look for' or 'search' in the correct form to finish the sentences.

1. *I saw customs officers _______________ the guy from America.*
2. *I _______________ that book, but I couldn't find it.*
3. *A helicopter was used to ___________ for the missing criminal.*
4. *It's like _______________ a needle in a haystack.*
5. *He's _______________ a new flat.*

127. Once, twice or three times?

Wrong *I go swimming one time per week.*
Right *I go swimming **once** a week.*

Erklärung

Die Wörter ‚einmal' und ‚zweimal' haben im Englischen in der Regel die unregelmäßigen Entsprechungen **‚once'** und **‚twice'**. Ab ‚dreimal' wird die Formel ‚Zahl + times' benutzt (‚three times'). ‚Once', ‚twice' und ‚… times' werden verwendet, um über regelmäßige Ereignisse zu sprechen und auf die Frage ‚wie oft?' zu antworten:

*How often do you go swimming? – **Once** a week?*
*How often do you eat out? – **Twice** a month.*
*How often do you go on holiday? – **Three times** a year.*

Practice makes perfect

Answer the following questions using 'once', 'twice' or '… times'.

How often do you do sport? ***Twice** a week.*

1. *How many times have you been on a foreign holiday?* ______________
2. *How often do you watch TV?* ______________
3. *How often do you go to concerts?* ______________
4. *How many times have you swum in the sea?* ______________
5. *How often do you read books?* ______________

128. All the time or every time?

Wrong *Our website is updated every time.*
Right *Our website is updated* ***all the time****.*

Erklärung

‚every time' heißt ‚jedes Mal':
He hits the green ***every time****.*
‚all the time' heißt ‚regelmäßig', ‚ständig' oder ‚andauernd':
He practices golf ***all the time****.*

Practice makes perfect

Choose the correct expression ('every time/all the time') to finish the sentences, as in the example.

Petrol prices are increasing ***all the time****/~~every time~~.*

1. *She drinks all the time/every time.*
2. *All the time/every time I see him he's with a different woman.*
3. *All the time/every time we raise our prices, turnover falls.*
4. *He keeps a gun by his bed all the time/every time.*
5. *He complains all the time/every time.*

129. Pension or retirement?

Wrong *I can't wait to go into pension.*
Right *I can't wait **to go into retirement/to retire**.*

Erklärung

Und schon wieder ein falscher Freund! Geht man in Rente, erhält man auf Englisch **‚a pension'** und ist **‚a pensioner'** (ein Rentner).
Die deutsche Pension dagegen (das Gasthaus) ist auf Englisch ein ‚guesthouse' oder ‚B&B' (‚bed and breakfast').
Will man auf Englisch sagen, dass man in Rente geht, heißt es **‚(to) retire'** oder **‚(to) go into retirement'**.
Außerdem muss man aufpassen, ‚Rente' niemals mit ‚rent' (Miete) zu verwechseln!
Beispiele:

*Bob's stopped work, he's **a pensioner** now.*
*I would like **to retire** next year.*
*Erica is looking forward to her **retirement**.*
*Rob doesn't get much of **a pension**.*

Practice makes perfect

Match a word from the explanations above to the descriptions below.

1. *A person who has stopped his/her working life.* ____________________
2. *To stop working.* ____________________
3. *Monthly amount paid by the government.* ____________________
4. *Leisure time after a working life.* ____________________
5. *A monthly amount paid for a flat, etc.* ____________________

130. By or on foot?

Wrong *It's not far, let's go by foot.*
Right *It's not far, let's go **on foot**.*

Erklärung

Auf Englisch heißt es immer:
***by** car/**by** plane/**by** taxi/**by** bike/**by** train*
ABER:
***on** foot*

Practice makes perfect

How do you get to the following places?

1. *School/work* ________________
2. *The airport* ________________
3. *Town* ________________
4. *A foreign country* ________________
5. *The kiosk on the corner* ________________

131. Crys or cries?

Wrong *She crys herself to sleep because she's so sad.*
Right *She **cries** herself to sleep because she's so sad.*

Erklärung

Ein leicht vermeidbarer Flüchtigkeitsfehler! Wenn ein Wort, das auf **‚y'** endet, an vorletzter Stelle einen Konsonanten hat, führt das Anfügen eines **‚s'** dazu, dass die Endung in **‚ies'** umgewandelt wird:

*I **cry** when I watch sad films, my wife **cries**.*
*I only have one **hobby**, but my brother has 10 **hobbies***
*One of my favourite **cities** is Gothenburg.*

Practice makes perfect

Use the words in brackets in the correct form to write sentences, as in the example.

(try/he/hard/school)	*He **tries** hard at school.*
1. *(one/hobby/fishing)*	______________________
2. *(she/study/history)*	______________________
3. *(fly/she/Rome/every summer)*	______________________
4. *(two/copy/my new book)*	______________________
5. *(three/baby)*	______________________

132. To or too?

Wrong *I didn't buy the car, it was to expensive.*
Right *I didn't buy the car, it was **too** expensive.*

Erklärung

‚too' wird verwendet, um einen Überschuss an etwas zu beschreiben (‚zu viel'):

__too many__ – We have __too many staff__.
__too much__ – It costs __too much__.

Als Adverb ist es Ausdruck einer Übertreibung:

That's __too__ expensive!
He was driving __too__ fast.

‚too' hat außerdem die Bedeutung ‚auch':

You are going to the match? Me __too__.
There was a clown at the party, __too__.

‚to' wird vor allem für Richtung und Bewegung verwendet:

I'm going __to__ Scotland next week.
Steve's going __to__ the shop, do you need anything?

Practice makes perfect

Finish the sentences using 'to' or 'too'.

1. *I suppose it's _____ much to ask?*
2. *_____ many people in our company don't care about their work.*
3. *When we got _____ the hotel, it was closed.*
4. *Is your sister coming _____ the party, _____?*
5. *_____ much water was pumped into the system.*

133. The?

Wrong *We are flying to the Heathrow Airport.*
Right *We are flying to* ***Heathrow Airport****.*

Erklärung

Flughäfen brauchen keinen bestimmten Artikel (‚the'), weil sie in der Regel nach Städten oder Regionen einer Stadt benannt werden.
Orte und Dinge, die Namen von Städten oder Menschen im Titel tragen, brauchen in der Regel ebenfalls kein ‚the':

JFK Airport, Cambridge University, Carnegie Hall

Genauso ist es bei Namen von Geschäften:

Macy's, Harrods, Bloomingdales

In all diesen Fällen fungieren die Namen als Eigennamen (wie Länder oder Personen) und sind klar identifizierbar (es gibt eben nur einen Flughafen mit dem Namen Heathrow).
Hotels hingegen brauchen ‚the'. Sie sind nicht klar unterscheidbar, da es viele Hotels gibt. Weil man von einem der vielen möglichen Hotels spricht, definiert man mit dem Artikel, von welchem Hotel genau man spricht:

The Hilton Hotel, The Sheraton

Practice makes perfect

Finish the sentences using the information above, as in the example.

When we went to New York we flew ***into JFK Airport****.*

1. *We flew out of* ______________________________.
2. *We stayed at* ______________________________.
3. *We shopped at* ______________________________.
4. *On the way back we had a stopover at* ____________________.
5. *But we didn't have time to shop at* ____________________.

134. This or these?

Wrong *I don't like this people.*
Right *I don't like **these** people.*

Erklärung

‚**this**' wird für die Einzahl verwendet:

> ***This** pencil is blunt.*
> ***This** film is terrible.*

‚**these**' ist die Pluralform:

> ***These** chips are cold.*
> ***These** CDs don't belong to me.*

Practice makes perfect

Write a reaction to the situation, as in the example.

You are in a restaurant, your steak is raw.
*Excuse me, **this** steak is not cooked.*

1. *An angry mob has gathered outside the Town Hall.*

   ____

2. *Your pen is dry.*

   ____

3. *You have a lot of problems.*

   ____

4. *The band you are watching is fantastic.*

   ____

5. *Your beer is warm.*

   ____

135. A jeans or jeans?

Wrong *I need a new jeans.*
Right *I need* ***new jeans.****/I need* ***a new pair of jeans****.*

Erklärung

Dinge, die aus zwei Teilen bestehen, stehen immer im Plural und werden als Plural behandelt: **‚jeans'** (zwei Beine), **‚trousers'** (zwei Beine) und genauso **‚glasses'** (Brille), **‚scissors'** (Schere), **‚shorts'** (kurze Hose), **‚pyjamas'** (Schlafanzug), **‚tights'** (Strumpfhose), **‚trunks'** (Badehose).

I like these ***jeans****.*
I want those ***glasses****.*
These ***shorts*** *are horrible.*

Man kann deshalb auch jeder Zeit **‚a pair of …'** sagen:

a pair of *jeans*
a pair of *trousers*
a pair of *glasses*
a pair of *shorts*

Will man sich auf mehrere solcher Plurale beziehen, muss man die Formulierung **‚x pairs of …'** verwenden:

two pairs of *glasses*

‚a/an' sind Singularartikel und deshalb nicht notwendig.

Practice makes perfect

Use the vocabulary above, in the correct form, to answer the questions.

What do I need to cut paper? ***A pair of scissors.***

1. *What should I wear on the beach?* ________________
2. *What do you wear in bed?* ________________
3. *What do you wear in winter under your pants?* ________________
4. *What should I wear when I can't see properly?* ________________
5. *What do I need, if I go swimming?* ________________

136. Capital letters? (1)

Wrong *i went to bonn with syd and karen.*
Right ***I** went to **Bonn** with **Syd** and **Karen**.*

Erklärung

Großbuchstaben werden für die folgenden Wörter bzw. Wortgruppen verwendet:
‚I' – (egal, wo es im Satz steht)
Namen (Eigennamen, Menschen, Städte)
__Barry__ lives in __Hong Kong__ now.
Tage
See you on __Monday__.
Monate
We won't see each other until __December__.
Länder
Let's go to __Japan__, I have never been there.
Sprachen
Do you speak any __French__?
Nationalitäten
I think he's __Croatian__, but I'm not sure.

Practice makes perfect

Decide if the following sentences are right or wrong, as in the example.

My birthday is in __March__. Right

1. *You never listen to a word I say.* ________
2. *We did french at school, I hated it!* ________
3. *Is the market on Saturdays?* ________
4. *Is your mother coming tomorrow?* ________
5. *It's your Birthday soon, isn't it?* ________

137. It's a tag, isn't it?

Wrong *You don't smoke, don't you?*
Right *You **don't** smoke, **do you**?*

Erklärung

‚question tags' folgen immer dem Muster:
negativ → positiv
positiv → negativ

*You **like** me, **don't** you?*
*You **don't** like me, **do** you?*
*He **can't** swim, **can he**?*
*She **will** come, **won't** she?*

Practice makes perfect

Choose the correct tag to finish these sentences, as in the example.

*Tom won't be late, **will he**?*

1. *It's getting late, ____________?*
2. *You couldn't lend me some money, ____________?*
3. *You're very brown, ____________?*
4. *I shouldn't have lost my temper, ____________?*
5. *He'd never met her before, ____________?*

138. Unpolite or impolite?

Wrong *Her new boyfriend is so unpolite.*
Right *Her new boyfriend is so **impolite**.*

Erklärung

Um Adjektive zu negieren, werden Präfixe verwendet, normalerweise ‚un-', aber es gibt eine Reihe von Ausnahmen. Hier hilft nur Auswendiglernen, um Fehler zu vermeiden!

*He is a very **impolite** man.*

Andere Beispiele:

*It's **impossible**.* – *NICHT: unpossible*
*He's very **immature**.* – *NICHT: unmature*
*He's very **immodest**.* – *NICHT: unmodest*

Practice makes perfect

Use the correct prefix to turn these words into the negative.

1. relevant	________________	*2. able*	________________
3. organized	________________	*4. treated*	________________
5. believable	________________	*6. happy*	________________
7. sure	________________	*8. reasonable*	________________
9. regular	________________	*10. safe*	________________

139. Have or had?

Wrong *We went to Africa last year, we have never been there before.*
Right *We went to Africa last year, we **had** never been there before.*

Erklärung

Spricht man über ein Ereignis in der Vergangenheit und bezieht sich dann auf etwas, das noch vor dieser Zeit lag, muss man die sog. Vorvergangenheit verwenden: Die Zeit heißt auf Deutsch Plusquamperfekt, auf Englisch **‚past perfect'** und wird gebildet, indem man ‚had' mit der 3. Form des Verbs kombiniert:

*I saw a French film yesterday, I **had** never **seen** it before.*
*I went to Italy last year, I **had been** there before in 1987.*

Practice makes perfect

Finish the sentences using the past perfect and the verb in brackets.

*(steal) When I got home last night, someone **had stolen** my garden gnome.*

1. *(eat)*
   I ate sushi last night, ______________________________.
2. *(ride)*
   We rode camels when we were in Egypt, ______________________.
3. *(speak)*
   I spoke to a Japanese guy at the airport, ____________________.
4. *(take)*
   I took a painkiller last night, __________________________.
5. *(choose)*
   I got picked for the football team today, ____________________.

140. Auxiliary verb or not?

Wrong *He should works harder.*
Right *He should **work** harder.*

Erklärung

Der Merkspruch ist bekannt: ‚he/she/it ein s muss mit' – aber nicht nach einem Hilfsverb!

*He **plays** squash. – He **can't play** squash.*
*She **speaks** Chinese. – She **might speak** Chinese.*
*He **saves** a lot of money. – He **could save** a lot of money.*

Practice makes perfect

Rewrite the sentences using the auxiliary verb in the brackets.

*My boss speaks Norwegian. My boss **can speak** Norwegian.*

1. *(should)*
   My brother drinks less. ______________________________

2. *(cannot)*
   My mum cooks. ______________________________

3. *(might)*
   Vera goes on holiday in August. ______________________________

4. *(should)*
   Wilma goes to bed early. ______________________________

5. *(cannot)*
   My English teacher explains grammar clearly. ______________________________

141. Make or take a photo?

Wrong *Louise always makes a lot of photos on holiday.*
Right *Louise always **takes** a lot of photos on holiday.*

Erklärung

***(to) make** a cake*
***(to) make** a plan*
***(to) make** an appointment*
***(to) make** a mistake*
ABER:
***(to) take** a photo!*

Practice makes perfect

Finish the sentences using 'make' or 'take' in the correct form.

*He **took** about 300 photos at the concert last week.*

1. *I'm __________ a cake for Billy's birthday.*
2. *I __________ so many mistakes in my exam, I must be stupid.*
3. *They are __________ plans for their holiday in Italy in the summer.*
4. *Have you __________ an appointment at the dentist's yet?*
5. *I have never __________ a picture of my car.*

142. Irregular verbs?

Wrong *Rose and Carl have splitted.*
Right *Rose and Carl* ***have split****.*

Erklärung

Viele Fehler entstehen, wenn man bei unregelmäßigen Verben ein ‚ed' anhängt! Dabei bleiben diese Verben in verschiedenen Zeitformen oft unverändert:

cut – cut – cut
split – split – split
bet – bet – bet
quit – quit – quit
hit – hit – hit

Man muss diese Formen auswendig lernen!

Practice makes perfect

Complete the graph.

Simple present	Simple past	Past participle
	hurt	
hide		
		bitten
seek		
	let	

143. Hour or hours?

Wrong *One and a half hour.*
Right *One and a half* ***hours****.*

Erklärung

Die einfachste Regel für den Plural auf Englisch ist das Pural-s! Trotzdem wird es oft vergessen, weil man entweder denkt, es könnte ein Singular sein, oder weil es auf Deutsch wie ein Singular aussieht. Korrekt sind immer nur diese Formen:

*one and a half week**s***
*two and half hour**s***
*one of my brother**s***
*two of my teacher**s***
*two euro**s***

Practice makes perfect

Answer the questions, as in the example.

What is 90 minutes? — *One and a half* ***hours****.*

1. *What is 90 seconds?* ______________________
2. *What is 45 days?* ______________________
3. *What is 730 days?* ______________________
4. *What are 20 years?* ______________________
5. *What are 200 years?* ______________________

144. Citys or cities?

Wrong *Paris is one of my favourite citys.*
Right *Paris is one of my favourite **cities**.*

Erklärung

Wörter mit ‚y' am Ende verändern manchmal ihre Schreibweise, wenn sie in der dritten Person Singular (‚he/she/it') oder im Plural verwendet werden.
Die Regel lautet: Steht vor dem **‚y'** ein Vokal (a, e, i, o, u), ändert das **‚s'** die Schreibweise nicht:

verbs	**nouns**
play – plays	*boy – boys*
say – says	*ray – rays*

Steht vor dem ‚y' ein Konsonant, wird die Endung ‚ies' geschrieben:

verbs	**nouns**
try – tries	*country – countries*
cry – cries	*city – cities*

Practice makes perfect

Use the words below in the correct form to finish the sentences.

hobby – boy – country – baby – story

1. *Little Stevie loves bedtime* ______________.
2. *Badminton is one of my* _____________.
3. *I haven't visited many foreign* _____________.
4. *Two little* ___________ *threw stones at my cat.*
5. ___________ *are fine, when they are asleep.*

145. Do or doing?

Wrong *I can imagine to do that.*
Right *I can **imagine doing** that.*

Erklärung

Einige Verben fordern von einem nachfolgenden Verb immer die **ing-Form**:

*He could never **imagine learning** Chinese.*
*Could you **stop doing** that?*
*I don't **remember saying** that.*
*He **regrets doing** that.*
*I'll **continue learning** French.*
*I **gave up asking** him.*
*I am **looking forward to hearing** from you.*

Practice makes perfect

Describe the situation on the left using the expressions above, as in the example.

Julia is really sorry about her behavior. *She **regrets doing** it.*

1. *Parachuting is not for me.* ______________________________
2. *Paul is not stopping his language course.* ______________________________
3. *Will you stop tapping your nails on the table, please!* __________________
4. *I've invited him four times already, not again.* _________________________
5. *Are you sure I agreed to that?* __________________________

146. Some or any?

Wrong *I have any friends.*
Right *I have **some** friends.*

Erklärung

‚**some**‘ wird in der Regel in positiven Sätzen verwendet:
*I got **some** nice presents for my birthday.*
*There is **someone** on the phone for you.*
‚**any**‘ wird vor allem in verneinten Sätzen und bei Fragen verwendet:
*I don't need **any** help.*
*She doesn't have **any** friends.*
*Do you have **any** brothers and sisters?*
*Did you catch **any** fish?*

Practice makes perfect

Complete the sentences using 'some' or 'any'.

1. *I've got ________ books about dinosaurs.*
2. *Natalia hasn't got ________ friends in Athens.*
3. *I don't think there are ________ palm trees in Britain.*
4. *Have you got __________ games for your computer?*
5. *There are ________ messages for you.*

147. As or than?

Wrong *Roy is bigger as you.*
Right *Roy is bigger **than** you.*

Erklärung

Vergleicht man zwei **gleiche** Dinge oder Personen, verwendet man **‚as … as'** (‚so … wie'):

*I'm **as** big **as** you.*

*This juice is **as** cheap **as** that one.*

Werden zwei ungleiche Dinge oder Personen miteinander verglichen, benutzt man **‚than'** (‚als'):

*He's fatter **than** me!*

*She's prettier **than** me.*

Practice makes perfect

Complete the sentences using 'as' or than'.

1. *New York is much bigger* _______ *Paris.*
2. *Is London more expensive* _______ *Rome?*
3. *I think Belgium is the same size* _______ *Holland.*
4. *The prices in Munich are higher* ________ *in Frankfurt.*
5. *Is Sweden* ______ *big* _______ *Norway?*

148. By or at?

Wrong *At the weekend I was by my mother-in-law.*
Right *At the weekend I was* **at** *my mother-in-law's.*

Erklärung

‚by' wird nie für Besuche benutzt! Stattdessen verwendet man **‚at'**:
I was ***at my sister's house.***
I was ***at my parents' house.***
Oft wird der eigentliche Ort auch weggelassen und es gilt die Formel Person + Apostroph = Ort:
I was ***at my sister's.***
I was ***at my parents.***
WICHTIG:
Bei Pluralformen auf ‚s' fällt das ‚s' nach dem Apostroph weg:
my sister's bedroom (eine Schwester)
my ***sisters'*** *bedroom (zwei oder mehr Schwestern)*

Practice makes perfect

Use an apostrophe to describe where the people are, as in the example.

Sue's having a haircut. Sue's ***at the hairdresser's.***

1. *Dad's gone to buy bread.* ______________________________
2. *Mum's gone for a check-up.* ______________________________
3. *Dick's having a tooth pulled.* ______________________________
4. *Natalia's visiting her mum and dad.* ______________________________
5. *Rick's gone to see his twin sister.* ______________________________

149. Engaged or committed?

Wrong *She is very engaged to her job.*
Right *She is very **committed** to her job.*

Erklärung

Achtung, falscher Freund!
Das englische Wort **‚engaged'** entspricht dem deutschen ‚verlobt':

*They are **engaged** to be married.*
*They announced their **engagement** last week.*

‚engaged' heißt außerdem ‚besetzt', wenn man telefoniert:

*The line was **engaged**.*

Dagegen ist jemand, der sich ‚engagiert' oder ‚Engagement zeigt', sich also mit viel Hingabe und Aufwand einer Sache widmet, auf Englisch **‚committed'**:

*He's very **committed** to his family.*
*She's very **committed** to the company.*
*They both show a lot of **commitment**.*

Practice makes perfect

Use the words above in the correct form to complete the sentences, as in the example.

*Ricky asked me if I wanted to get **engaged**.*

1. *Did they invite you to the ______________ party?*
2. *His ______________ leaves a lot to be desired.*
3. *He's not very ______________, is he?*
4. *Did you get ______________ before you got married?*
5. *She doesn't show much ______________.*

150. Floor or corridor?

Wrong *There's a photocopier in the floor if you need one.*
Right *There's a photocopier* ***in the corridor*** *if you need one.*

Erklärung

Achtung, falscher Freund!
Auch **‚floor'** verursacht nur deshalb Probleme, weil es wie ein deutsches Wort klingt (nämlich ‚Flur'), aber etwas ganz anderes bedeutet:

floor = *Fußboden*
corridor = ***Flur***

Practice makes perfect

Use 'floor' or 'corridor' to complete the sentences.

1. *Put the cartons on the __________ in my office.*
2. *He's always standing in the __________ gossiping.*
3. *They've taken the drinks machine out of the __________.*
4. *There's a big hole in my __________ carpet.*
5. *He was standing in the __________ the last time I saw him.*

151. Fast or fastly?

Wrong *He runs really fastly.*
Right *He runs really* ***fast****.*

Erklärung

Einige Wörter sind verwirrend, weil sie als Adjektive und Adverbien gleich geschrieben werden (also unregelmäßig sind):

He's a ***fast*** *runner.*
He runs ***fast****.*
She's a ***hard*** *worker.*
She works ***hard****.*
He's a ***late*** *arrival.*
He's working ***late****.*

Nicht vergessen:

hardly = *kaum*
lately = *in letzter Zeit*

Practice makes perfect

Choose the correct word to finish the sentences.

1. *I haven't seen Phil late/lately.*
2. *He does hardly/hard any work when the boss is out of the office.*
3. *He was over three hours lately/late and didn't even apologize.*
4. *It was all over very fast/fastly!*
5. *He came very late/lately.*

152. Mobile or handy?

Wrong *Can I use your handy for a minute?*
Right *Can I use your **mobile phone** for a minute?*

Erklärung

Niemand ist sich wirklich sicher, warum das englische Wort ‚handy' (auf Deutsch ‚praktisch') verwendet wird, um ein Mobiltelefon zu beschreiben! Es gibt noch weitere solcher eingedeutschten Wörter, die im Englischen eine andere Bedeutung haben:

He doesn't check what I'm saying.
*– He doesn't **understand** what I'm saying.*
I never liked putting puzzles together.
*– I never liked putting **jigsaws** together*
They are mobbing my daughter at work.
*– They are **harassing** my daughter at work.*

Practice makes perfect

Use the correct words to describe the situations on the left, as in the example.

*Wilma needs to make an urgent phone call. She needs to borrow a **mobile phone**.*

1. *Kathy's getting a new superior next week.* ______________________
2. *Fred hates Chinese food.* ______________________
3. *Candy can cook really well.* ______________________
4. *She finds his manner very offensive.* ______________________
5. *Tom's preparing some food.* ______________________

153. Send or broadcast?

Wrong *Sat 1 sent a great programme about nuclear energy last night.*
Right *Sat 1 **broadcast** a great programme about nuclear energy last night.*

Erklärung

Im Deutschen kann man für die beiden Bedeutungen ‚ausstrahlen' und ‚verschicken' dasselbe Wort ‚senden' benutzen. Im Englischen braucht man zwei verschiedene Wörter:
‚to broadcast' oder **‚to show'** für ausgestrahlte Filme, Serien etc.,
‚to send' für verschickte Lieferungen oder übermittelte Wünsche:

*Did you **send** Auntie Jan a birthday card?*
*Paul **sends** his best wishes.*
*BBC **broadcast** a new Sherlock last night.*

Practice makes perfect

Describe the situations on the left using 'send', 'show' or 'broadcast' in the correct form, as in the example.

*Paul's at the post office buying a stamp. He's sending someone a **birthday card.***

1. *Sat 1 have got 20 cameras at the match.* ____________________
2. *The BBC are planning a new series about apes.* ____________________
3. *Say hello to Mary for me.* ____________________
4. *Don't forget grandma's birthday!* ____________________
5. *Kathy got two Valentine's cards.* ____________________

154. Want or wants?

Wrong *It depends what other people wants.*
Right *It depends what other people **want**.*

Erklärung

Wenn man über mehrere Personen oder Dinge spricht, benötigt ‚(to) want' kein ‚s' am Ende:

*What do the kids **want** for Christmas?*
*What do the boys **want** to eat?*

Ein ‚s' wird nur in der dritten Person Singular angehängt:

*The dog **wants** a bone.*
*Little Susie **wants** an ice-cream.*

Practice makes perfect

Choose 'want' or 'wants' to finish the sentences, as in the example.

*Wendy ~~want~~/**wants** a new bike for Christmas.*

1. *Some people just do not know what they want/wants.*
2. *He want/wants something to eat.*
3. *Harry's not happy at work, he want/wants more money.*
4. *They said they want/wants to rent the room.*
5. *Somebody want/wants you on the phone, they didn't give their name.*

155. Proud or pride?

Wrong *He' so full of proud.*
Right *He's so full of **pride**.*

Erklärung

Substantiv und Adjektiv soll man nie verwecheln!

__Pride__ makes people __proud__.
__Bravery__ makes people __brave__.
__Happiness__ makes people __happy__.

Practice makes perfect

Choose the correct word (noun/adjective) to finish the sentences!

*Brian was so full of **pride**/~~proud~~ when he collected his medal.*

1. *Are you pride/proud of what you've done?*
2. *He had to be very bravery/brave to do what he did.*
3. *There was a lot of glamour/glamourous at the awards ceremony.*
4. *She was very kind/kindness to the kids.*
5. *She showed a lot of bitter/bitterness towards him after they split up.*

156. Overhours or overtime?

Wrong *I have to work a lot of overhours at the moment.*
Right *I have to work a lot of* ***overtime*** *at the moment.*

Erklärung

Viele Wörter, die mit Arbeit zu tun haben, werden falsch gebraucht:

(to) ***do*** *work*	*– NICHT: (to) make*
(to) do or work ***overtime***	*– NICHT: overhours*
(to) work ***long hours***	*– NICHT: overhours*
(to) ***have*** *or* ***take*** *breaks*	*– NICHT: (to) make*
full-time *or* ***part-time*** *jobs*	*– NICHT: half-day*
the ***boss*** *of the company*	*– NICHT: chef*

Practice makes perfect

Choose the correct word from above to describe the sentences on the left, as in the example.

Phil's the Managing Director. *He's the* ***boss****.*

1. *Sally only works four hours a day.* ______________________
2. *Graham's been working late every night this week.* ______________________
3. *Beate does a 38-hour week.* ______________________
4. *Rick's in the canteen.* ______________________
5. *I usually do 12-hour shifts.* ______________________

157. Talk or discuss?

Wrong *We were discussing about the new project.*
Right *We were **discussing/talking about** the new project.*

Erklärung

Verwendet man **‚discuss'**, ist ‚about' nicht mehr notwendig. Benutzt man hingegen ‚talk', muss man **‚talk about'** daraus machen. Weitere Verben in diesem Zusammenhang sind:

*(to) **argue about** something (über etwas streiten)*
*(to) **confess to** something (etwas gestehen)*
*(to) **ramble on about** something (faseln, schwafeln, nicht auf den Punkt kommen)*
*(to) **rant on about** something (faseln, schwafeln, sich aufregen über)*
*(to) **admit to** something (etwas zugeben)*

Practice makes perfect

Choose the correct expression from above to describe the situation.

*Ron said it was his fault. He **admitted** to doing it.*

1. *She never stopped talking.* ______________________________
2. *They had a disagreement about the price.* ______________________________
3. *We had a long discussion about the problem.* ______________________________
4. *Joe was very upset and loud and wouldn't shut up!* ______________________________
5. *The robber admitted to committing the crime.* ______________________________

58. Game or play?

Wrong *It was a really exciting football play.*
Right *It was a really exciting football **game**.*

Erklärung

‚**(to) play**' ist ein Verb und beschreibt eine Handlung:

*Let's **play** football.*

*Let's **play** cards.*

‚**a play**' (Substantiv) ist ein Theaterstück:

*We watched the Shakespeare **play** at the Lyric Theatre in London.*

‚**a game**' ist ein Spiel für zwei oder mehr Personen oder zwischen Mannschaften:

*Did you see the United **game** last night?*

*Do you want a **game** of Monopoly?*

Practice makes perfect

Use 'play' or 'game' in the correct form to finish the sentences, as in the example.

*How many ~~plays~~/**games** are left in the season?*

1. *Did you get a part in the school __________?*
2. *Have you ever __________ for your country?*
3. *He's written three __________ but had no success so far.*
4. *To some people life is just a __________.*
5. *He __________ the __________ with a protective mask yesterday.*

159. Most or the most?

Wrong *The most time I stay at home at the weekends.*
Right ***Most of** the time I stay at home at the weekends.*

Erklärung

Vor den folgenden Formulierungen ist der bestimmte Artikel ‚the' nicht notwendig:

> ***Most of** the people in my office are lazy.*
> ***Most of** the time I ride my bike to work.*
> ***Most of** the money from the sale of the house is gone.*

Hingegen ist ‚the' beim Superlativ unerlässlich:

> ***The most visited country** in the world is France.*
> ***The most famous player** in the world is Messi.*
> ***The most expensive city** in England is London.*

Practice makes perfect

Use 'most of' or 'the most' to describe the sentences on the left, as in the example.

*It's one o'clock in the morning, the party's almost over. **Most of** the guests have gone.*

1. *There is almost no ice in the fridge.* ________________________

2. *Beijing has a high level of pollution.* ________________________

3. *Paris is a popular tourist destination.* ________________________

4. *I have no one to spend the weekend with.* ________________________

5. *I don't like my teammates.* ________________________

160. His, her or their?

Wrong *I heard Robbie lost their job?*
Right *I hear Robbie lost* ***his*** *job?*

Erklärung

‚his/her/its' sind die Possessivpronomina zu **‚he/she/it'** (Singular):

They threw him out because ***his*** *dog barks all night.*

She doesn't know how to control ***her*** *kids.*

‚their' wird nur für den Plural, als Possessivpronomen zu **‚they'** verwendet:

Paul and Lesley are selling ***their*** *house.*

They sold all ***their*** *shares and bought a boat.*

Practice makes perfect

Use 'their', 'his' or 'her' to finish the sentences, as in the example.

She said it wasn't ***her*** *fault.*

1. *Don't tell him, let him use _______ brain for once!*
2. *_______ car broke down and they had to walk for miles to get to a garage.*
3. *_______ house is always messy, he lives like a pig!*
4. *_______ mother left him a lot of money in her will.*
5. *I don't like _______ style of management.*

161. Side or page?

Wrong *It was on the front side of the newspaper.*
Right *It was on the **front page** of the newspaper.*

Erklärung

Zeitungen und Zeitschriften haben **‚pages'** (NICHT: ‚sides' wie auf Deutsch):

*I always read the fashion **page** first.*

*How many **pages** does your newspaper have?*

Weitere Tipps: Artikel oder Nachrichten stehen ‚in the newspaper' (NICHT: ‚at' oder ‚on'):

*Is there a TV guide **in the newspaper**?*

ABER: **‚on a page'**:

***On** which page is the crossword?*

Practice makes perfect

Answer the questions using the information above, as in the example.

Where did you read that story? ***In the newspaper.***

1. *Where can I find last night's football results?* ______________________
2. *Where can I read about models?* ______________________
3. *Where do you usually print the headlines?* ______________________
4. *Where are the sports headlines?* ______________________
5. *Where will they print my correspondence?* ______________________

162. Call or call to?

Wrong *I called to the office to tell them I was sick.*
Right *I **called** the office to tell them I was sick.*

Erklärung

Manchmal ist es einfacher als man denkt! Jemanden ‚anrufen' heißt lediglich **‚(to) call someone'**:

*I **called** the police because I didn't like the look of the man who was hanging around.*

*I **called** Sue to wish her all the best for her journey.*

Andere Beispiele für ein Zu-viel-des-Guten:

(to) go home	– NICHT: *(to) go to home*
the week after next	– NICHT: *the week after next week*
two o'clock	– NICHT: *two o'clock p.m.*
near a city	– NICHT: *in the near*

Practice makes perfect

Answer the questions using the information above, as in the example.

What do you do when you've finished work? ***I go home.***

1. *What do you do if you want to speak to someone on the phone?*

   ____

2. *What time do you usually get up?* ______________________________
3. *Close to which big city do you live?* ______________________________
4. *What would you do in an emergency?* ______________________________
5. *What did you do the last time you finished school/work?*

   ____

163. Lucky or happy?

Wrong *I was really lucky when they told me I'd got the job.*
Right *I was really **happy** when they told me I'd got the job.*

Erklärung

Es ist so leicht, diese Wörter zu verwechseln! Hier der Unterschied:
'happy' bedeutet 'glücklich', man ist zufrieden mit etwas, man hat Glücksgefühle:

*I'm very **happy** with the way things are going at the moment.*
*I am so **happy** you came to visit me.*

'lucky' dagegen bedeutet 'Glück haben':

*I was really **lucky** to get the last ticket for the concert.*

Practice makes perfect

Decide if the following situations are 'lucky' or 'happy'.

1. *You find €20 lying in the street.* ________________
2. *You mishit your shot, but it hits another player and goes into the net.*

   ____
3. *A hole in one on the golf course.* ________________
4. *Lying next to your partner on a tropical beach.* ________________
5. *All your plans are working out.* ________________

164. Have or not?

Wrong *I have been to London last Saturday.*
Right *I **went** to London last Saturday.*

Erklärung

Diese beiden Zeitformen auseinanderzuhalten ist nicht leicht!
‚I have been' wird ohne festen Zeitpunkt in der Vergangenheit benutzt (‚present perfect'):

I have been to Spain many times.

‚I went' wird mit festem Zeitpunkt in der Vergangenheit verwendet (‚simple past'):

I went to Spain in 2013.

Practice makes perfect

Choose the correct word to finish the sentences.

1. *I have rode/ridden a camel many times.*
2. *Last night my brother has been/went to the cinema.*
3. *I went/have been to Ibiza many times.*
4. *We went/have been to Italy last year.*
5. *Did you go/have you been to the concert on Friday?*

165. Decide on or for?

Wrong *We decided for Alan.*
Right *We **decided on** Alan.*

Erklärung

Entscheidet man sich für jemanden/etwas, heißt es auf Englisch **,to decide on** someone/something':

*It was between Alan and Tom, in the end we **decided on** Tom.*

*It was between Spain and Tunisia. In the end we **decided on** Tunisia.*

Für das Gegenteil benutzt man **,to decide against** someone/something':

*We've **decided against** building an extension.*

Sich zu etwas entschließen hingegen heißt **,to decide to do** something':

*We've **decided to** get married.*

Practice makes perfect

Use the correct expression to finish the sentences.

1. *Pat had to go to prison because the jury* ________________ *him.*
2. *We* ________________ *paint the kitchen blue after all.*
3. *It was a hard decision to make, but we've finally* ______________ *Sicily.*
4. *He suddenly* ______________ *go.*
5. *We've* ________________ *climb Mount Everest.*

166. Devil's circle?

Wrong *There is no solution, it's a devil's circle.*
Right *There is no solution, it's **a vicious circle**.*

Erklärung

ACHTUNG: Viele Wörter oder Ausdrücke können nicht direkt ins Englische übersetzt werden!

Kaiserschnitt	= *Caesarian section*
Mutterschaftsurlaub	= *maternity leave*
Hochzeitstag	= *wedding anniversary*
Kindergeld	= *family allowance*
Notausgang	= *emergency exit*

Practice makes perfect

Use the correct expression to finish the sentences.

1. *Iris has just had a baby, she's on* ____________________.
2. *She spends the* ____________________ *on gin and cigarettes.*
3. *There was a mad rush for the* ________________ *when the fire broke out.*
4. *He can't get a job, so he drinks because he's depressed, it's*

   ____________________.
5. *Mum and dad are celebrating their 50th* ____________________.

167. Black and white or white and black?

Wrong *The film was in white and black.*
Right *The film was in **black and white**.*

Erklärung

Viele mehrgliedrige Ausdrücke sind feststehende Begriffe und haben eine feste Reihenfolge:

*Do you have any **brothers and sisters**?*
*They are so different, they're like **chalk and cheese**. (wie Kalk und Käse, also Tag und Nacht)*
*Life has its **ups and downs**.*
*Little jobs like that are my **bread and butter**.*
*We are not staying at a hotel, we're staying at a **bed & breakfast**.*
*Are you sitting comfortable, **boys & girls**? Then I'll begin …*

Practice makes perfect

Use one of the expressions above to finish the sentences.

1. *How those two ever got together I will never know, they are like*

   ________________________.

2. *Do you have any* ____________________________*?*
3. *We found a nice* ________________________ *down by the lake.*
4. *My plumber friends always tell me that other people's sewage is his*

   ________________________________.

5. *Our company has had its* _______________________, *but things are ok now.*

168. Note or notice?

Wrong *I made a notice of it in my diary.*
Right *I made **a note** of it in my diary.*

Erklärung

‚**a notice**' steht meistens an irgendeiner Wand:

*They put the details on the **noticeboard** in the entrance.*
*There's **a notice** hanging in the corridor about this year's AGM.*
(AGM = annual general meeting)

‚**(to) notice**' ist das Verb und bedeutet ‚etwas bemerken'. Englische Synonyme sind ‚to see' oder ‚to be aware of':

*I **notice** you've bought a new car.*
*I **noticed** him in the lift, but he didn't speak.*

‚**a note**' ist etwas, das man aufschreibt, also eine Notiz:

*I made **a note** of his details.*
*I left **a note** on his desk.*

Man kann auch eine ‚***mental note***' von etwas machen, also ohne Stift und Zettel.

Practice makes perfect

Use 'note' or 'notice' in the correct form to finish the sentences.

1. *I suggest you all make __________, I'll only say this once.*
2. *Did you __________ the looks on all the faces when he came into the room?*
3. *I didn't read the __________ you left for me, what did it say?*
4. *When she ______________ I was watching her, she started blushing.*
5. *I made a ____________, then forgot all about it.*

169. In former times or I used to?

Wrong *In former times I lived in Frankfurt.*
Right ***I used to** live in Frankfurt.*

Erklärung

Der Ausdruck **‚used to'** wird für Dinge verwendet, die man früher gemacht hat, jetzt aber nicht mehr:

***I used to** play a lot of football, but I'm too old now.*
***I used to** really like him, but he's a boring fool nowadays.*
***I didn't use to** smoke so much.*
***I didn't use to** be so grumpy.*

Practice makes perfect

Use 'used to' or 'didn't use to' and the words in brackets to write about your past.

1. *(football)* ______________________
2. *(study hard)* ______________________
3. *(pessimistic)* ______________________
4. *(live at home)* ______________________
5. *(drink alcohol)* ______________________

170. Know or knowing him?

Wrong *I have been knowing him for 25 years.*
Right *I have **known** him for 25 years*

Erklärung

Einige Verben haben keine ing-Form:

*I **believe** you*	*– NICHT: I am believing you*
*I **love** you*	*– NICHT: I am loving you*
*I **remember** you*	*– NICHT: I am remembering you*
*I **regret** it*	*– NICHT: I am regretting it*
*I **hate** you*	*– NICHT: I am hating you*
*It **belongs** to me*	*– NICHT: it is belonging to me*

Practice makes perfect

Use the correct form of the verb in brackets above to write a reply!

*Hi, it's Paul Johnson, isn't it? – Hey, Steve Jones, I **remember** you from school!*

1. *What do you think of our new CEO? (hate)* ______________________________
2. *You left your last company, now we're closing down. (regret)* ______________________________
3. *I used to be in the SAS. (believe)* ______________________________
4. *Whose is the Porsche parked outside? (belong)* ______________________________
5. *How long have you known your wife? (known)* ______________________________

171. Neighbour or neighbouring?

Wrong *My brother lives in the neighbour village.*
Right *My brother lives in the **neighbouring** village.*

Erklärung

Was ursprünglich ing-Form war, ist oft ein eigenes neues Wort! Man muss es als solches lernen und darf vor allem auf falsche Freunde nicht hereinfallen:

*He lives in the **neighbouring** town or village.*
*I like **doing** something – playing football for example.*
*air **conditioning***
*Football is **interesting**. (NICHT: interested)*
*This is a **non-smoking** carriage.*
*I am **listening** to you.*
*I get paid at the **beginning** of the month.*

Practice makes perfect

Answer the questions using the information above.

1. *When does your best friend live?* ______________________
2. *What are you doing?* ______________________
3. *What do you like doing?* ______________________
4. *What do you find interesting?* ______________________
5. *How do hotels keep the rooms cool?* ______________________

172. Smoke or smoking?

Wrong *Are you still smoking?*
Right ***Do you still** smoke?*

Erklärung

‚do you …' wird verwendet, um nach Tatsachen oder regelmäßigen Handlungen zu fragen:

> ***Do you** smoke?*
> ***Do you** still live in West Street?*
> ***Do you** see anybody from school these days?*

‚are you … + -ing' fragt nach Aktivitäten, die jetzt gerade oder in der Zukunft geschehen:

> ***Are you** still waiting for that phone call?*
> ***Are you** going out tonight?*

Practice makes perfect

Answer the questions using complete sentences.

1. *Do you smoke?* ______________________________
2. *Are you smoking now?* ______________________________
3. *Do you still see people you were at school with?* ______________________________
4. *Are you going on holiday soon?* ______________________________
5. *Do you go on a winter holiday?* ______________________________

173. Relaxeder?

Wrong *He seems relaxeder these days.*
Right *He seems **more relaxed** these days.*

Erklärung

‚er' wird an kleine, also einsilbige Adjektive angehängt:
*small – **smaller***
*big – **bigger***
‚more …' braucht man für Adjektive, die aus zwei oder mehr Silben bestehen:
*relaxed – **more** relaxed*
*relaxing – **more** relaxing*
*important – **more** important*
Einzige Ausnahme sind zweisilbige Adjektive, die auf ‚y' enden, dann wird aus dem ‚y' ein ‚i':
*lazy – **lazier***
*early – **earlier***

Practice makes perfect

Write sentences using the words in brackets and suitable adjectives!

*(Rolls Royce/Mini) A Rolls Royce is **more expensive** than a Mini.*

1. *(Paris/Bonn)* ______________________________
2. *(a laptop/a desktop)* ______________________________
3. *(snack bar/Japanese restaurant)* ______________________________
4. *(cigarettes/cigars)* ______________________________
5. *(jogging/hiking)* ______________________________

174. Fair priced?

Wrong *It was fair priced.*
Right *It was fairly-priced.*

Erklärung

Das Partizip Perfekt (**past pasticiple**, die dritte Form des Verbs) braucht immer ein Adverb, um näher beschrieben zu werden:

*write, wrote, **written*** – *The book was **well-written**.*
*speak, spoke, **spoken*** – *He is **softly-spoken**.*
*take, took, **taken*** – *The goal was **well-taken**.*

Practice makes perfect

Use the adverb-adjective combination to describe the following things as in the example:

an inexpensive sweater. *An inexpensive sweater is **reasonably-priced**.*

1. *a good book* ______________________________

2. *a boring book* ______________________________

3. *a quiet person* ______________________________

4. *a brilliant goal* ______________________________

5. *an educated man* ______________________________

175. Ice bears?

Wrong *Did you see the ice bears at the zoo?*
Right *Did you see the* ***polar bears*** *at the zoo?*

Erklärung

Achtung, falscher Freund! Vermeide immer direkte Übersetzungen:

Eisbär – ***polar bear***
Eis – ***ice-cream*** *(NICHT: ice)*

Nützliche Eis-Ausdrücke sind:

(to) break the ice – *das* ***Eis*** *brechen*
(to) put on ice – *auf* ***Eis*** *legen, kalt stellen*
(to) de-ice. – ***enteisen***

Practice makes perfect

Use the words/expressions to write responses.

1. *We've put off the expansion until next year.* ______________________
2. *I'm hot!* ______________________
3. *My car has been outside all night.* ______________________
4. *I went to the zoo yesterday.* ______________________
5. *I don't know anyone who is coming to the party.* ______________________

176. At or on the airport?

Wrong *Rick's on the airport, he's picking Mum up.*
Right *Rick's* ***at the airport****, he's picking Mum up.*

Erklärung

‚on the airport' bedeutet wörtlich ‚auf dem Dach des Flughafens'. Das ist nicht erlaubt! **‚at'** wird für Orte und Ereignisse verwendet:

at *home*
at *the city hall*
at *Christmas*

Practice makes perfect

Describe where the following people are.

1. *Bill is waiting in the departure lounge.* ____________________
2. *Jan is queuing outside a concert hall.* ____________________
3. *Sue and Sam are watching a new film.* ____________________
4. *The children are swimming in the sea.* ____________________
5. *Ronnie is having a haircut.* ____________________

177. Way or direction?

Wrong *I think the company is on the right way.*
Right *I think the company is* ***going in the right direction.***

Erklärung

Achtung, falscher Freund! Für den Ausdruck ‚auf dem richtigen Weg sein', also für die Einschätzung einer Situation oder für Pläne, verwendet man immer **‚direction'**:

We are going ***in the right direction.***

‚way' kann für die Art, etwas zu tun oder zu behandeln, und für Routen eingesetzt werden:

Is Bob doing that ***in the right way?***

Excuse me, can you tell me ***the way to Newport?***

In nicht übertragener Bedeutung wird **‚direction'** natürlich auch für Wegbeschreibungen benutzt:

You're going in the wrong direction. Turn round and go in the ***direction of the motorway.***

Practice makes perfect

Use 'way' 'or 'direction' to finish the sentences.

1. *It's easy, you just have to do it in the right* ________________.

2. *Is this the* ________________ *to the town hall?*

3. *We've been through a bad period, but I think we are going in the right*

________________ *now.*

4. *Ask the policeman the* ________________ *to the M6.*

5. *Left or right? Which* ________________ *shall we go?*

178. Didn't talk or talked?

Wrong *We didn't talked about it last night.*
Right *We **didn't talk** about it last night.*

Erklärung

Verneint man ein Verb mit ‚to do' (in den Formen **‚don't'**, **‚doesn't'** und **‚didn't'**), steht danach immer der Infinitiv des Vollverbs:

We watch TV a lot. – *We **don't watch** TV a lot.*
He likes cooking. – *He **doesn't like** cooking.*
We went to the party after all. – *We **didn't go** to the party after all.*

Practice makes perfect

Change the following sentences into negative sentences, as in the example.

*Tom likes meeting new people. Tom **doesn't like** meeting new people.*

1. *Irene cooks hot meals for Nick.* ______________________________

2. *They like each other.* ______________________________

3. *He really cares about his appearance.* ______________________________

4. *We believe in global warming.* ______________________________

5. *I like your style.* ______________________________

179. Talking or am talking?

Wrong *I talking to Bob on the other line, can I call you back?*
Right ***I am talking** to Bob on the other line, can I call you back?*

Erklärung

Die ing-Form wird niemals ohne ‚is/are/am' verwendet! Umgekehrt werden für das ‚present progressive' ‚is/are/am' niemals ohne die ing-Form des Verbs verwendet. Sie sind ein Team!

FALSCH: He running. – FALSCH: He is run.

Die Regel lautet: **present progressive** = ing-Form des Verbs + is/are/am

*Jasmine **is watching** the film.*
*You **are getting** on my nerves.*
*I **am going** now, see you soon!*

Practice makes perfect

Write present progressive sentences using the words in brackets!

*(they/argue/TV) **They are arguing** about which TV programme to watch.*

1. *(Neil/drive/fast)* ____

2. *(Police/criminals/robbery)* _________________________________

3. *(band/record/new songs)* __________________________________

4. *(bake/cake)* ____

5. *(climb/Everest)* ____

180. Look forward to?

Wrong *I look forward to meet you next week.*
Right *I look forward to* ***meeting*** *you next week.*

Erklärung

Diesen Fehler findet man ständig in Briefen und E-Mails! Der Ausdruck **‚to look forward to'** zieht immer ein Verb in der **ing-Form** nach sich:

I look forward ***to meeting you in August****.*
I look forward ***to getting your invitatio****n.*

Ebenfalls möglich ist diese Form:

I ***am looking forward to*** *doing something.*
I ***am looking forward to*** *going on holiday.*
Lou ***is looking forward to*** *retiring in six months.*
Mum and dad ***are looking forward to*** *seeing their first grandchild*

Practice makes perfect

Write sentences about yourself using the words in brackets, as in the example.

(holiday) I am looking forward to ***going*** *on holiday in Spain.*

1. *(finish/work)* ______________________________
2. *(meet/friends)* ______________________________
3. *(see/family)* ______________________________
4. *(drive/new car)* ______________________________
5. *(see/children)* ______________________________

181. Job or work?

Wrong *My girlfriend has got a new work.*
Right *My girlfriend has got **a new job**.*

Erklärung

‚**work**' ist unzählbar und braucht keinen unbestimmten Artikel (‚a/an'):

*I have **so much work** to do.*
*I did **all that work** you asked me to do.*
*My boss doesn't seem very happy **with my work**.*

‚**job**' ist ein zählbares Substantiv in der Einzahl und benötigt daher den Artikel ‚**a**':

*I've got **a job** at last!*
*Did Paul get **a job** at the new supermarket?*
*It's not **a very good job**, but the money is not too bad.*

Practice makes perfect

Use 'job' or 'work' in the correct form to finish the sentences, as in the example.

*Bricklaying is really hard **work**.*

1. *Tony's got a ___________ which she really does not like.*
2. *I do all the ___________ and he gets all the credit!*
3. *Your ___________ is not very satisfactory.*
4. *Do you think your ___________ is safe?*
5. *There isn't much ___________ around these days.*

182. The police?

Wrong *The police is coming.*
Right *The police **are coming**.*

Erklärung

Wenn man von einer Behörde oder anderen staatlichen Institution spricht, verwendet man in der Regel den Plural:

> ***The police are** doing a good job.*
> ***The government have** changed the immigration laws again.*
> ***The army are** recruiting again.*
> ***The Foreign Office have** ignored public opinion and deported the asylum seekers.*

Practice makes perfect

Choose 'is/are' to finish the sentences.

1. *A foreign office official is/are giving a press conference this afternoon.*
2. *The policeman is/are facing trial for corruption.*
3. *The police is/are moving in to stop the rioting.*
4. *The government is/are considering their options.*
5. *The army is/are deploying more soldiers in Afghanistan.*

183. I will?

Wrong *I promise I call you next week.*
Right *I promise **I will** call you next week.*

Erklärung

Für Entscheidungen oder Abmachungen wird immer das ‚will future' verwendet:

*I **will send** you the prices tomorrow.*
*Ok, I **will come** to the concert with you on Saturday.*
*I promise I **will get back** to you tomorrow.*

Practice makes perfect

Write a response using the will future.

1. *There's no sugar left.* ______________________________
2. *I need that certificate for school.* ______________________
3. *It's mum's birthday tomorrow.* _________________________
4. *It's raining.* ____________________________________
5. *The plumber rang again asking about his money!* ___________

184. Success or successful?

Wrong *He is really success.*
Right *He is really **successful**.*

Erklärung

Substantiv oder Adjektiv? Sie werden oft durcheinandergebracht!

*He's had **success**.* – *He is really **successful**.*
*She's introduced a lot of **innovation**.* – *She incredibly **innovative**.*
*You have to admire his **creativity**.* – *He's really **creative**.*

Practice makes perfect

Complete the chart.

noun	**adjective**
beauty	
	miserable
	strong
violence	
	kind

185. Life or the life?

Wrong *The life is hard.*
Right ***Life** is hard.*

Erklärung

Manchmal ist ‚the' nicht erforderlich, man spricht ganz allgemein von einer Sache oder von etwas, das nicht weiter bestimmt werden muss:

***Life** gets harder as you get older.*
***Global warming** is a serious threat to our environment.*
*I love **nature**.*
***Central Park** is right in the middle of New York.*
***Globalisation** brings the world closer together.*

‚the' kann verwendet werden, um deutlich zu machen, dass man über eine ganz bestimmte Sache spricht, z. B. über ein ganz bestimmtes Leben oder über *die* Chinesische (und nicht irgendeine) Mauer:

***The life of an immigrant** is hard.*
***The parks in London** are wonderful.*
***The United States** has a lot of national parks.*
***The Great Wall of China** is amazing.*

Practice makes perfect

Choose the correct expression to finish the sentences.

1. *He always dreamed of life/the life in another country.*
2. *It's a different way of life/the life in the outback.*
3. *I'm really worried about the effects of the global warming/global warming.*
4. *Did you go to Hyde Park/the Hyde Park when you were in London?*
5. *We are destroying nature/the nature with pollution.*

186. Self or selves?

Wrong *The kids cooked the dinner themself.*
Right *The kids cooked the dinner* ***themselves****.*

Erklärung

Reflexivpronomina im Plural brauchen ein **‚ves'** am Ende:
Singular: myself – yourself – himself – herself – itself
*Plural: oursel**ves** – yoursel**ves** – themsel**ves***

Practice makes perfect

Use the correct reflexive pronoun to finish the sentences.

1. *Jim treated ____________ to a new jumper.*
2. *He nearly wet ____________ when the dog jumped over the fence.*
3. *If you don't look after ____________ you'll both get sick.*
4. *I'm not very keen on her ____________.*
5. *Leave it, let them do it ____________ if they think they are so clever!*

187. Its or it's?

Wrong *I think its going to rain tomorrow.*
Right *I think **it's going** to rain tomorrow.*

Erklärung

‚it's' ist die Kurzform von **‚it is'** oder **‚it has'**:
*It is snowing. – **It's** snowing.*
*It is really expensive. – **It's** really expensive.*
‚its' dagegen ist ein Possessivpronomen und zeigt Zughörigkeit oder Besitz an:
*It's impossible to separate a dog from **its** bone!*
*The hotel has changed **its** policy regarding guests in the room.*

Practice makes perfect

Use 'it's' or 'its' to finish the sentences.

1. ______ *never easy to settle in a new town.*
2. *The petrol station has increased ______ prices again!*
3. ______ *got nothing to do with you!*
4. ______ *too late now!*
5. *He said ______ in the company's own interests.*

188. There or their?

Wrong *I don't like there new dog.*
Right *I don't like **their** new dog.*

Erklärung

Auch **‚their'** ist ein Possessivpronomen und zeigt an, dass jemandem etwas gehört:

*It's **their** own house.*

***Their** children are hideous.*

‚there' dagegen ist ein Demonstrativpronomen und heißt ‚da' oder ‚dort'. **‚there is'** bedeutet ‚es gibt':

*Put the dish over **there**.*

***There is** plenty of food in the kitchen.*

Practice makes perfect

Use 'there' or 'their' to finish the sentences.

1. ________ *are never enough toilets at these events.*

2. *It's* ________ *own fault, they wouldn't listen.*

3. ________ *is not much we can do about it now.*

4. *He said* ________ *bank has agreed to give them a mortgage.*

5. *When* __________ *au-pair leaves they'll have big problems.*

189. For or ago?

Wrong *We first met for 10 years.*
Right *We first met **10 years ago**.*

Erklärung

‚… years ago' gibt an, wie lange etwas Bestimmtes her ist (‚es geschah vor soundsoviel Jahren'):

*We got married **10 years ago**.*
*I left school **25 years ago**.*

‚for … years/hours/etc.' gibt an, wie lange etwas schon andauert oder gedauert hat:

*The dispute has been going on **for years***
*The meeting should go on **for about two hours**.*
*We talked **for hours** about old times.*

Practice makes perfect

Answer the following questions using 'for' or 'ago'.

1. *How long have you known your best friend?* ____________________
2. *When did you first meet him/her?* ____________________
3. *When did you first start learning English?* ____________________
4. *How long have you been learning English?* ____________________
5. *When did you start/leave school?* ____________________

190. Was or were?

Wrong *We was in town all afternoon.*
Right ***We were** in town all afternoon.*

Erklärung

Das **‚simple past'** von ‚(to) be' hat zwei Formen, **‚was'** und **‚were'**:
Der Singular ist ‚was' (Ausnahme ‚you were').
Der Plural ist ‚were'.

*I **was** – he **was** – she **was** – it **was***
*you **were** – we **were** – they **were***

Practice makes perfect

Use 'was' or 'were' to finish the sentences.

1. *Pete and Mary ________ engaged for 11 years before they got married.*
2. *Jenny and I _______ trapped in a lift for two hours yesterday.*
3. *How long ________ you at the party for?*
4. *It ________ not the result I'd been expecting.*
5. *Everyone ________ shocked when she left him for another woman.*

191. Get up or stand up?

Wrong *I usually stand up for work at six.*
Right *I usually **get up** for work at six.*

Erklärung

Verben mit bestimmten Präpositionen **(‚phrasal verbs')** unterscheiden sich im Deutschen und Englischen meistens. Also Vorsicht vor falschen Freunden!

*(to) **get up** in the morning (aufstehen)*
***Stand up** if you don't want to sit down anymore! (sich hinstellen)*
*(to) **take off** clothes or shoes (ausziehen)*
*(to) **put on** clothes or shoes (anziehen)*
*(to) **pick** someone **up** at the airport (abholen)*
*(to) **drop** someone **off** at the station (absetzen)*
*(to) **turn** the volume **up** or **down** (leiser oder lauter stellen)*
*(to) **turn** something **on** or **off** (an- oder ausschalten)*
*(to) **put** something **down** (hinlegen, weglegen)*

Practice makes perfect

Use the correct phrasal verb, in the correct form, to finish the sentences.

1. *I ________ Mum ______ at the airport in plenty of time to get her plane.*
2. *All the people in front of us were __________ _____. We couldn't see a thing.*
3. *He __________ ______ the radio and went to bed.*
4. *Can you ______ _____ the music? I can't hear myself think.*
5. *Leave that alone! ________ it _____!*

192. Whose or who's?

Wrong *Who's car is that?*
Right ***Whose** car is that?*

Erklärung

‚who's' ist die Kurzform von ‚who is':

Who is your boss? – ***Who's** your boss?*

Who is the man in the black coat? – ***Who's** the man in the black coat?*

‚whose' ist ein Interrogativpronomen und fragt nach dem Besitzer einer Sache (‚wessen?'):

***Whose** coat is that?*

***Whose** Porsche is that?*

Practice makes perfect

Use 'who's' or 'whose' to finish the sentences.

1. *I don't know __________ to blame.*

2. *I wonder ___________ making all that noise.*

3. *___________ version do you believe?*

4. *Do you know _________ putting up the money?*

5. *__________ that women standing against the wall?*

193. Waiting or waitting?

Wrong *I've been waitting for over an hour now.*
Right *I've been **waiting** for over an hour now.*

Erklärung

Manchmal muss der letzte Buchstabe eines Wortes verdoppelt werden. Dies geschieht in der Regel, wenn das Wort auf **Vokal + Konsonant** endet:

*(to) shop – **shopped – shopping***
*(to) jog – **jogged – jogging***
*(to) run – **running***
*big – **bigger***
*thin – **thinner***

Diese Regel gilt nicht, wenn vor dem Konsonanten zwei Vokale stehen:

*(to) wait – **waited – waiting***
*(to) need – **needed – needing***
*cheap – **cheaper***

Practice makes perfect

Use the words in brackets in the correct form to finish the sentences!

*(hot) It's the **hottest** July on record.*

1. *(feed) Little Jilly loves ___________ the ducks in the park.*
2. *(hop) He ___________ on one leg all the way down the street.*
3. *(big) Is London ___________ than Newcastle?*
4. *(sun) Look at that lazy dog! ___________ himself on the balcony.*
5. *(reap) He ___________ the rewards of his hard work.*

194. Easy or easily?

Wrong *We can do that easy.*
Right *We can do that **easily**.*

Erklärung

Verwende immer ein Adverb, um ein Verb näher zu beschreiben!

*We should do it **quickly**.*
*He always works so **slowly**.*
*You should listen **carefully**.*

Practice makes perfect

Describe how you do the following things, as in the example.

*(eat) I usually eat really **quickly**.*

1. *(drive)* ____________________________________
2. *(talk)* ____________________________________
3. *(drink alcohol)* ______________________________
4. *(get angry)* ________________________________
5. *(give blood)* _______________________________

195. Take or make?

Wrong *He's lazy. He just won't take the effort to do his job properly.*
Right *He's lazy. He just won't* ***make*** *the effort to do his job properly.*

Erklärung

‚make' und **‚take'** werden gerne verwechselt! **‚(to) make an effort'** heißt ‚sich bemühen, sich anstrengen, Willen zeigen', ‚sich die Mühe machen' heißt dagegen ‚(to) go to the trouble of'. Hier weitere Beispiele, was wozu gehört:

(to) ***make*** *a will/a sandwich/progress/a break/a breakthrough*
(to) ***take*** *a holiday/your time/a break/liberties/stock*

Practice makes perfect

Match a definition on the left with an expression from above!

Put all your energy into something. ***Make*** *an effort.*

1. *Prepare some food.* ______________________
2. *Have a rest.* ______________________
3. *Review your current situation.* ______________________
4. *Work slowly.* ______________________
5. *Experience success.* ______________________

196. Mean or think?

Wrong I mean he's lazy.
Right I ***think*** he's lazy.

Erklärung

Zwei Wörter, die ebenfalls oft verwechselt werden, sind **‚mean'** und **‚think'**:

‚I think …' heißt ‚Ich bin der Meinung, dass …'.

‚I mean …' heißt ‚Ich will damit sagen, dass …'.

__I think__ he can't do the job. – I am of the opinion that he can't do the job.

You are coming with me. No, not you – __I meant__ the other guy!

‚meaning' heißt ‚Bedeutung':

What is the __meaning__ of this letter?

‚Meinung' heißt **‚opinion'**:

What is your __opinion__ of the new government?

Practice makes perfect

Use 'mean', 'think', 'opinion' or 'meaning' in the correct form to finish the sentences.

1. *That's not what I ________ and you know it!*
2. *He _________ he's the right man for the job, I'm not so sure.*
3. *Do you understand the _____________ of the words?*
4. *In my ___________ we don't stand a chance!*
5. *He ___________ he could just walk in here and change everything.*

197. Of or to?

Wrong *I don't know the solution of the problem.*
Right *I don't know the **solution to** the problem*

Erklärung

Nicht immer benutzt man im Englischen dieselbe grammatische Konstruktion oder dieselbe Präposition!

*the **solution to** the problem (die Lösung des Problems)*
*the **answer to** the question (die Antwort auf die Frage)*
*a **question of** time (eine Frage der Zeit)*
*a **matter of fact** (eine Tatsache)*
*a **fact of life** (die harte Wirklichkeit)*

Practice makes perfect

Match an expression from above to a sentence on the left, as in the example.

*Kay will be here any minute now. It's a **question** of time.*

1. *This is my reply.* ____________________
2. *That's the honest truth.* ____________________
3. *That's the key.* ____________________
4. *I do this all the time.* ____________________
5. *The rich get richer, the poor get poorer.* ____________________

198. Work?

Wrong *I'm going to the cinema after the work.*
Right *I'm going to the cinema* ***after work****.*

Erklärung

Das englische **‚work'** wird immer ohne bestimmten Artikel benutzt und ist unzählbar!

I'm ***at work****.*	*– NICHT: at the work/on the work*
success ***at work***	
after ***work***	*– NICHT: after the work*
Do you have ***much work****?*	*– NICHT: many work*

Practice makes perfect

Use the correct word to finish the sentences, as in the example.

He always goes for a drink ***after work****.*

1. *Did you ring Roy when you got home ______ work?*
2. *He's not ____ work today, he's got a day off.*
3. *There's not _______ work around here since the factory closed down.*
4. *I always need breakfast before I go ____ work.*
5. *Please don't phone me ____ work.*

199. By or from?

Wrong *He was attacked from a tiger.*
Right *He was attacked* ***by a tiger****.*

Erklärung

Wird in Passivkonstruktionen der Urheber oder Handelnde erwähnt, muss man auf Englisch **‚by'**, benutzen:

*   ***attacked by*** *something*
*   *a book or record (written or recorded)* ***by*** *someone*

Geht es um Zeit, Ort oder Richtung heißt es **‚from'**:

*   *a person* ***from*** *another country*
*   ***from*** *another planet*
*   *a letter* ***from*** *someone (wenn es darum geht, dass jemand ihn geschickt hat)*

Practice makes perfect

Use 'by' or 'from' to finish the sentences.

1. *He was savaged ____ a vicious dog.*
2. *She said she saw a creature ______ outer space.*
3. *Have you got any LPs ____ Fleetwood Mac?*
4. *I think he said he's ______ Italy.*
5. *He got a postcard ______ his parents in Spain.*

200. On or in?

Wrong *Life can be very stressful for people on high-level jobs.*
Right *Life can be very stressful for people* ***in high-level jobs****.*

Erklärung

Welche Präposition wo verwendet wird, muss man leider auswendig lernen!

'in' heißt es bei Job oder Arbeit:

in the job
in a certain position
in a certain department

'on' oder **'at'**, wenn auf der Arbeit von einem bestimmten Niveau die Rede ist:

at a high level
on a high level
on a different level

Aber Achtung! Bei oder in einer Bank zu arbeiten, heißt:

(to) work ***for*** *a bank*

Practice makes perfect

Use 'in', 'on' or 'at' to finish the sentences.

1. *He doesn't behave very well for a man ____ his position.*
2. *Which department are you ____?*
3. *Are we ____ the same wavelength?*
4. *Are you ____ work at the moment?*
5. *It's a different world ____ management level.*

201. Is born or was born?

Wrong *I am born in Canada.*
Right *I **was born** in Canada.*

Erklärung

Nicht vergessen! Mit den Zeiten nehmen es die Engländer genau: Was in der Vergangenheit geschah, muss auch in der Vergangenheit stehen. Dabei wird **‚am/is'** in der einfachen Vergangenheit zu **‚was'.**
‚are' wird in der einfachen Vergangenheit zu **‚were'**.
Und ganz wichtig: ‚borned' ist leider völlig falsch!

Practice makes perfect

Describe the sentences on the left using 'is/are/am/was/were' as in the example.

Last night Ron and Joan went to town.
*Last night Ron and Joan **were** in town.*

1. *He's from Scotland.* ______________________________
2. *We went to Spain last year.* __________________________
3. *I come from England.*______________________________
4. *Rick and Sam go out together.* ________________________
5. *Rick nearly lost an eye!*____________________________

202. Present

Wrong *I have to presentate our new product tomorrow.*
Right *I have to* ***present*** *our new product tomorrow.*

Erklärung

Verwenden Sie keine Wörter, die nicht existieren, auch wenn sie dem Deutschen noch so ähnlich klingen:

(to) present	*– NICHT: presentate (für: präsentieren)*
(to) reserve	*– NICHT: reservate (für: reservieren)*
(to) remind someone to do something	*– NICHT: remember (für: erinnern)*
fast	*– NICHT: fastly*
more expensive	*– NICHT: more expensiver*

Practice makes perfect

Use the words in brackets and the correct words from the explanation to build sentences.

1. *(a hotel room for Jim)* ______________________________

2. *(dad's birthday)* ______________________________

3. *(champagne/sparkling wine)* ______________________________

4. *(my new sports car)* ______________________________

5. *(next year's budget)* ______________________________

203. Hire or rent?

Wrong *We've hired a holiday flat for two weeks in June.*
Right *We've* ***rented a holiday flat*** *for two weeks in June.*

Erklärung

‚**(to) rent**' kann für jede Art von Ausleihe oder Buchung benutzt werden, egal ob Fahrrad, Auto, Haus oder Wohnung.
‚**(to) hire**' wird nur für das Leihen eines Fahrrads, Autos oder anderen Fahrzeugs verwendet.

Practice makes perfect

Use 'hire' or 'rent' in the correct form to finish these sentences.

1. *They've ________ a huge villa to celebrate their golden wedding anniversary.*
2. *In Venice we _________ a gondola, it was really expensive.*
3. *We _________ motorbikes to ride around Sicily.*
4. *Are you __________ your flat or did you buy it?*
5. *Jack has to _______ a big van to move flat.*

204. Afraid of or about?

Wrong *Are you afraid about snakes?*
Right *Are you* ***afraid of*** *snakes?*

Erklärung

Präpositionen, Präpositionen! Welche auf Englisch gebraucht werden, muss man auswendig lernen:

afraid of *something*
scared of *something*
terrified of *something*
worried about *something/someone*
thinking about *something*
wondering about *something*

Practice makes perfect

Use the expressions above to describe the sentences on the left, as in the example.

You won't get Mike on the big wheel! He's ***terrified of*** *heights.*

1. *Why is Bob so nervous?* ______________________________
2. *I've heard the sales figures are really bad again.* ________________
3. *Are you going to accept their offer of compensation?* ____________
4. *Pick it up, it won't bite you!* ____________________________
5. *They are making 20 people redundant.* _____________________

205. For or ago?

Wrong *I started at the company for three years ago.*
Right *I started at the company* ***three years ago****.*

Erklärung

‚for' + Zeit beschreibt einen Zeitraum (‚ago' hat in dieser Formulierung nichts zu suchen):

I've been here ***for three hours****.*

Zeit + **‚ago'** beschreibt einen Zeitpunkt (‚Wie lange ist es her?'):

I came about ***three hours ago****.*

‚ago' steht immer am Ende des Satzes.

Practice makes perfect

Answer the questions on the left, using 'for' or 'ago', as in the example.

How long have you been reading this book? **For** *two hours.*

1. *When did you get up today?* ____________________
2. *When did you last see your best friend?* ____________________
3. *How long do you usually sleep?* ____________________
4. *When did you last go on holiday?* ____________________
5. *How long have you lived in your present home?* ____________________

206. Word order (1)

Wrong *He spoke very well English.*
Right *He **spoke English** very well.*

Erklärung

Satzbau! In der Regel werden Verb und Objekt von Adverbien nicht getrennt:

*speak/German – He **speaks German** really well.*
*play/tennis – He **plays tennis** brilliantly.*
*talk/plant – He **talks to his plants** intimately.*

Practice makes perfect

Use the words in brackets to build a sentence using the correct word order, as in the example.

*(early/go home/he) He always **goes home** early.*

1. *(well/write/poems)* ______________________________

2. *(see/Val/lately)* ______________________________

3. *(exercise/regularly)* ______________________________

4. *(easy/test/pass)* ______________________________

5. *(well/play/we)* ______________________________

207. Word order (2)

Wrong *He uses always a dictionary to do his homework.*
Right *He **always uses** a dictionary to do his homework.*

Erklärung

Satzbau! Die Subjekt-Objekt-Verbindung wird von Adverbien wie **‚always/never/sometimes'** etc. getrennt. Diese Adverbien stehen immer vor dem Verb:

*I **usually go** home at six.*
*I **never stay out** late during the week.*

Wird das Prädikat aus Verb + Hilfsverb gebildet, steht das Adverb zwischen den beiden Verbteilen:

*I **don't usually stay** out late*
*I **can never understand** him.*

Practice makes perfect

Use the words in brackets to build a sentence using the correct word order, as in the example.

*(never/left//my wife) I **should never have left** my wife.*

1. *(stay/always/hotel)* ______
2. *(usually/Helen/help)* ______
3. *(need/don't/treatment)* ______
4. *(could/not/reach)* ______
5. *(not/usually/play/* ______

208. Hand or side?

Wrong *On the one side it's a great idea, on the other side it's risky.*
Right ***On the one hand** it's a great idea, **on the other hand** it's risky.*

Erklärung

Achtung, falscher Freund! Übersetzen Sie niemals direkt vom Deutschen ins Englische! Andere Beispiele sind:

*He's a good **electrician**.*	*– NICHT: electricker*
***happy** about something*	*– NICHT: lucky*
*on the one **hand** ... on the other **hand***	*– NICHT: side*
*(to) **donate** money to something*	*– NICHT: spend*
*(to) choose from the **menu***	*– NICHT: card*
*(to) **get** something*	*– NICHT: become*

Practice makes perfect

Use the correct words from above to complete the sentences.

1. *The _______________ put the plugs on the wrong wall.*
2. *He ____________ most of the money he won to charity.*
3. *He was so _____________, he started crying.*
4. *Where did you ______ that nice suntan?*
5. *There's nothing on the _________ I fancy.*

209. Wore or weared?

Wrong *I weared this dress yesterday, don't you remember?*
Right *I **wore** this dress yesterday, don't you remember?*

Erklärung

Unregelmäßige Verben haben eine eigene past-Form und brauchen kein ‚ed'! Andere häufige Fehler:

*catch – **caught** – NICHT: catched*
*take – **took** – NICHT: taked*
*drive – **drove** – NICHT: drived*
*eat – **ate** – NICHT: eated*

Practice makes perfect

Turn these sentences into the simple past using the correct irregular verb form.

1. *He breaks every toy he gets.* ____________________
2. *He dreams about sheep.* ____________________
3. *He sleeps like a baby.* ____________________
4. *The wind blows hard.* ____________________
5. *He rings the doorbell.* ____________________

210. Eastern or Easter?

Wrong *Are you going away on Eastern?*
Right *Are you going away **at Easter**?*

Erklärung

Achtung, Präpositionen!

***on** Friday*	*(für Wochentage!)*	*NICHT: at*
***at** Christmas*	*(für Feiertage!)*	*NICHT: on*
***on** my birthday*	*(für besondere Tage!)*	*NICHT: at*
***at** 10 o'clock*	*(für Zeitangaben!)*	*NICHT: on*

In den Beispielsätzen oben verbirgt sich außerdem ein falscher Freund: Gerne hängen wir an das englische ‚Easter' ein ‚n', weil es im Deutschen ‚Ostern' heißt.

Practice makes perfect

Answer the following questions using the correct time prepositions.

1. *When do you usually go shopping?* ____________________
2. *When do you get up for work?* ____________________
3. *When do you celebrate?* ____________________
4. *When are the cities full of bright lights?* ____________________
5. *When do the kids get chocolate eggs?* ____________________

211. Children or childrens?

Wrong *How many childrens do you have?*
Right *How many **children** do you have?*

Erklärung

Wörter, die bereits im Plural stehen, brauchen kein Plural-s! Andere Beispiele:

men – *NICHT: mens*
women – *NICHT: womens*
sheep – *NICHT: sheeps*
feet – *NICHT: feets*
teeth – *NICHT: teeths*
mice – *NICHT: mouses*

Practice makes perfect

Use the correct words from above to complete the sentences.

1. *The dentist had to give me a filling in one of my ______.*
2. *He follows her around like a ________.*
3. *He wears clothes that would look more suitable on ________.*
4. *I think we've got ______ in the cellar.*
5. *Not all ______ are macho.*

212. Build or build up?

Wrong *When I was in Costa Rica we built up two houses for the villagers.*
Right *When I was in Costa Rica we* ***built two houses*** *for the villagers.*

Erklärung

‚**(to) build**' bedeutet ‚etwas bauen', in der Regel ein Gebäude oder irgendeine Art von Infrastruktur:

They are ***building a new motorway****.*
My parents ***built this house*** *in 1989.*

‚**(to) build something up**' bedeutet ‚etwas über einen längeren Zeitraum aufbauen':

We have ***built up*** *a very good business over the last 10 years.*
Ron is ***building up*** *his muscles in the fitness studio.*

Practice makes perfect

Use 'build' or 'build up' in the correct form to complete the sentences.

1. *He's ____________ a loyal following over the last 25 years.*
2. *The traffic is ____________. It'll take hours to get home.*
3. *This particular model was __________ in 1934.*
4. *They are __________ a huge housing estate on the edge of town.*
5. *They had to completely re-________ the village after the hurricane.*

213. Used to doing something?

Wrong *My boyfriend is used to go to France on holiday.*
Right *My boyfriend is **used to going** to France on holiday.*

Erklärung

Eine Person, die es gewohnt ist, etwas zu tun, ist **‚used to doing something'**:

*She is **used to getting** her own way.*
*He is **used to sleeping** all day at the weekend.*
*I'm not **used to staying** out so late.*

Nicht zu verwechseln mit dem Satz **‚I used to …'**, um zu beschreiben, was jemand früher gemacht hat, jetzt aber nicht mehr:

*I **used to** smoke (but I don't now).*
*I **used to** live with my parents (but now I have my own place).*
*He **used to** go swimming (but now he plays tennis)*

Practice makes perfect

Describe the situation on the left using 'used to' in the correct way, as in the examples.

Her son is so spoilt. He is used to getting his own way.
*He's teetotal now. He **used to drink** a lot.*

1. *Her shouting doesn't bother him.* ______________________
2. *He doesn't see his friends anymore.* ______________________
3. *He can stand the smell.* ______________________
4. *She lived nearby, but she's moved.* ______________________
5. *He doesn't mind picking her up after work.* ______________________

214. In or on the countryside?

Wrong *I prefer living on the countryside.*
Right *I prefer living* ***in the countryside****.*

Erklärung

Für die meisten Orte wird **‚in'** verwendet:

I live ***in the countryside****.*
He lives ***in Spain****.*
She lives ***in Frankfurt****.*
They live ***in a big house****.*
Sue lives ***in a beautiful little village****.*

Ausnahmen sind z. B.:

on an island, on the planet, at the station.

Practice makes perfect

Use the words in brackets to write sentences about yourself.

1. *(Germany)* ______________________________
2. *(house/flat)* ______________________________
3. *(town/city/village)* ______________________________
4. *(countryside)* ______________________________
5. *(Europe/Asia)* ______________________________

215. Hours

Wrong *I sometimes spend hours in reading.*
Right *I sometimes* ***spend hours reading****.*

Erklärung

Auf ‚spend time' folgt immer die **ing-Form** (Gerundium): ‚(to) spend your time **doing** something':

I ***spend days looking*** *at old photos.*
I ***spend hours cooking*** *for my family.*
I ***spent my holiday touring*** *round Europe.*

Practice makes perfect

Describe how you spend your time, as in the example.

(hours) I spend hours ***watching*** *football.*

1. *(days)* ____
2. *(weeks)* ____
3. *(months)* ____
4. *(years)* ____
5. *(ages)* ____

216. Apprenticeship

Wrong *I made my apprenticeship at our Frankfurt plant.*
Right ***I did my apprenticeship** at our Frankfurt plant.*

Erklärung

Etwas tun heißt immer **‚(to) do'**, ‚(to) make' dagegen bedeutet ‚etwas erschaffen':

***(to) do** an apprenticeship*
***(to) do** advertising*
***(to) do** sport*
***(to) do** nothing*
***(to) do** someone a favour*
***(to) do** your best*

Practice makes perfect

Use 'do' in the correct form to complete the sentences.

1. *He _______ an apprenticeship as a plumber, then got a job driving a taxi.*

2. *Has she ________ the shopping?*

3. *They ________ a lot of advertising for the new product.*

4. *We've ________ our best, it's up to you now.*

5. *Can you ______ me a favour?*

217. In or on average?

Wrong *In average I go on holiday twice a year.*
Right ***On average** I go on holiday twice a year.*

Erklärung

‚on average‘ wird in diesem Fall wie ‚usually‘ verwendet, um auszudrücken, dass etwas ‚normalerweise‘ oder ‚gewöhnlich‘ so geschieht:

*I **usually** go on holiday twice a year.*

Andere Varianten sind:

*I **normally** do sport about twice a week.*
*I **generally** get up at about seven o'clock.*
***As a rule** I go to bed at about 11 o'clock.*
*We **typically** work in the garden on Sundays in the summer.*
*We **customarily** have a party on our wedding anniversary.*

Practice makes perfect

Use the words in brackets to write about yourself.

1. *(on average)*____
2. *(normally)* ____
3. *(as a rule)* ____
4. *(typically)*____
5. *(usually)*____

218. Affect of effect?

Wrong *The divorce had a really bad affect on her schoolwork.*
Right *The divorce had a really bad* ***effect*** *on her schoolwork.*

Erklärung

Achtung, nicht verwechseln!
‚(to) affect' ist ein Verb (‚beeinflussen'):
The recession ***affected*** *the way we work.*
‚effect' ist ein Substantiv (‚Auswirkung'):
This weather is having a terrible ***effect*** *on our crops.*

Practice makes perfect

Use 'affect' or 'effect' in the correct form to finish the sentences.

1. *Were you ____________ by the wave of redundancies?*
2. *There will be a knock-on ____________ of the local mill closing.*
3. *I think this recession ____________ all of us.*
4. *What were the after ____________ of the riots?*
5. *Try not to let the crowd __________ your concentration.*

219. There or they're?

Wrong *There closing the motorway to carry out repairs on Sunday.*
Right ***They're** closing the motorway to carry out repairs on Sunday.*

Erklärung

Klingt fast identisch, bedeutet aber etwas völlig anderes!
‚there‘ kann je nach Kontext z. B. ‚da, dort, dorthin‘ oder ‚es gibt‘ bedeuten:

__There__ is a traffic jam in the city.
Your hat and coat are __over there__.
Tom's in Spain? How did he get __there__?

‚they're‘ ist die Kurzform von ‚they are‘ und bezieht sich meist auf Menschen:

__They're__ putting up their prices again.
__They're__ refusing to comment about the rumours.

Practice makes perfect

Use 'they're' or 'there' to finish the sentences.

1. *_________ might be a surprise in store for you!*
2. *_________ not taking on any more staff at the moment.*
3. *I think I'll build my house over _________.*
4. *When _________ on holiday, they always lie on the beach.*
5. *_________ not telling the truth.*

220. Toys or toy's?

Wrong *Their children have so many toy's, it's unbelievable!*
Right *Their children have so many* ***toys****, it's unbelievable!*

Erklärung

Das Apostroph wird nie für den Plural verwendet!
The children have a lot of ***toys****.*
Es steht entweder vor dem Genitiv-s:
He plays with ***children's*** *toys.*
Oder ersetzt einen ausgelassenen Buchstaben (Elision):
Grandpa's *repairing her toys. (statt: Grandpa is)*
An Plurale, die nicht auf ‚s' enden, wird das Genitiv-s einfach mit Apostroph angehängt:
men's *toilets*
women's *clothes*
An Plurale, die auf ‚s' enden, wird nur das Apostroph angehängt:
a ***girls'*** *school*
an old ***folks'*** *home*

Practice makes perfect

Decide if the following sentences need an apostrophe or not. Place the apostrophe in the correct place if you think one is needed, as in the example.

Put the food in the mouses cage. *Put the food in the* ***mouse's*** *cage.*

1. *Ron has bought 20 pounds of food for his white mice.*
2. *Dad found a womans handbag on the train yesterday.*
3. *Those scissors are really sharp, be careful!*
4. *I need a new pair of trousers for work.*
5. *She went to a girls school.*

221. Then or than?

Wrong *Our new apartment is much bigger then the old one.*
Right *Our new apartment is much* ***bigger than*** *the old one.*

Erklärung

‚than' wird mit dem Komparativ verwendet und leitet den Vergleich ein (‚größer als'):

Our heating bills are much ***higher than*** *they used to be.*
Our new car is ***more economical than*** *the old one.*

‚then' hat immer mit Zeit zu tun und heißt ‚dann' oder ‚als nächstes':

We had just had the dishwasher fixed, ***then*** *the washing machine broke down.*
We called the police, ***then*** *the ambulance.*

Practice makes perfect

Choose the correct word ('then/than') to finish the sentences.

1. *Her new boyfriend is much older ______ I expected.*
2. *It's a lousy job, but it's better ______ nothing.*
3. ______ *we found out that the money had not been paid into our account.*
4. *Dad's doing ok, his temperature is lower ______ it was yesterday.*
5. *I think he's bit off more ______ he can chew!*

222. Compliments or complements?

Wrong *Our complements to the chef.*
Right *Our **compliments** to the chef.*

Erklärung

‚a compliment', **‚compliments'** oder **‚(to) compliment'** haben alle mit den netten Dingen zu tun, die wir über jemanden oder etwas sagen (Eselsbrücke: dt. ‚Kom**pli**ment' – engl. ‚com**pli**ment', beide mit ‚i'):

*He paid her a lot of nice **compliments**.*
*May I **compliment** you on the wonderful organisation?*

‚a complement' oder **‚(to) complement'** bedeutet, dass etwas zu etwas anderem gut passt (Eselbrücke: es ergänzt, kom**ple**tt macht, mit ‚e'):

*This wine **complements** the fish perfectly.*
*This piece is a wonderful **complement** to the other porcelain.*

Practice makes perfect

Use the correct word ('compliment/complement') in the correct form to finish the sentences.

1. *If that's a ________________, I wouldn't like to hear her insults.*
2. *Do you really think baked beans are the right kind of ________________ to salmon?*
3. ________________ *of the season to you all.*
4. *My mother sends her ________________.*
5. *He ________________ me on my new haircut.*

223. Advice or advise?

Wrong *She never asks for my advise.*
Right *She never asks for my **advice**.*

Erklärung

‚**(to) advise**' ist das Verb und beschreibt, was man tut (Aussprache mit weichem ‚s'):

*I would **advise** you to handle the situation very carefully.*
*I think you need an expert to **advise** you.*

‚**advice**' ist das dazugehörige Substantiv und beschreibt, was man braucht oder bekommt (Aussprache mit scharfem ‚s'):

*You need expert **advice**.*
*Take my **advice**, don't buy that car.*

Practice makes perfect

Use the correct word to finish the sentences.

1. *Maybe you should go to the Citizen's Advice/Advise Bureau?*
2. *My brother could advice/advise you, he's a lawyer.*
3. *I'm looking for some sound financial advise/advice.*
4. *It's my job as your bank manager to advice/advise you.*
5. *If you'd have listened to your parents' advice/advise, this would never have happened.*

224. Cancelled or delayed?

Wrong *My plane was cancelled by an hour.*
Right *My plane was **delayed by an hour**.*

Erklärung

‚cancelled' bedeutet ‚abgesagt, annulliert' – der Flug oder etwas anderes wird also nie stattfinden.

*They **cancelled** the Christmas party due to a lack of funds.*
*He's **cancelled** his German tour because ticket sales are so bad.*

‚delayed' bedeutet, dass etwas zu einem späteren Zeitpunkt stattfinden wird:

*My train was **delayed** because of a derailment.*
*We've **delayed** the publication by two weeks.*

Practice makes perfect

Decide if the following things are cancelled or delayed, as in the example:

We are meeting on Wednesday instead of Tuesday. *delayed*

1. *The summer fete has been scrapped.* ________
2. *Bob's train is an hour late.* ________
3. *We're going on holiday in autumn not summer.* ________
4. *He's staying in Madrid a while longer.* ________
5. *We shelved the idea of expansion.* ________

225. Make a trip?

Wrong *Shall we make a bike trip at the weekend?*
Right *Shall we* ***go on a bike trip*** *at the weekend.*

Erklärung

Achtung, falscher Freund! Spricht man über Ferien oder Kurzurlaube, verwendet man in der Regel die Verben **‚(to) take'** oder **‚(to) go on'**, nicht ‚(to) make':

You can take or go on a trip/a journey/a holiday/a sight-seeing tour/ a boat ride/a donkey ride/a safari/a bike ride/a walking holiday/ an adventure holiday, etc.

Practice makes perfect

Describe the sentences on the left, as in the example:

Julie is going to see the wild animals in Africa. She's ***going on*** *a safari.*

1. *Tommy saw a lot of museums and places in Stockholm.* ______________
2. *Helen went on the Rhine.* ______________
3. *Sid spent three weeks in Italy.* ______________
4. *Fred had problems with a stubborn mule.* ______________
5. *Lynn got wet through nearly every day.* ______________

226. Capital letters? (2)

Wrong *Did Roy send you that E-mail about the party?*
Right *Did Roy send you that **e-mail** about the party?*

Erklärung

Niemals Großbuchstaben für normale Substantive benutzen! Nur Eigennamen (**‚proper nouns'**) werden groß geschrieben:

*I called **Jodie** to help me in the garden.*
*She is going on a trip to **Paris** in summer.*

Practice makes perfect

Capitalise or de-capitalise the following sentences, as in the example.

kim and george got married last Week.
***Kim** and **George** got married last **week**.*

1. *Can you put it all in an E-mail?*

___

2. *The Hotel was Great.*

___

3. *Bruno sends his Love.*

___

4. *I bought the new rod Stewart Record. It's great!*

___

5. *Jill stayed at the Hilton for Two Nights.*

___

227. Don't forget the e!

Wrong *Someone has stolen my satellit dish.*
Right *Someone has stolen my **satellite** dish.*

Erklärung

Oft entstehen Fehler, weil am Endes des Wortes das ‚e' vergessen wird (meistens, weil es still ist, manchmal, weil es auf Deutsch dort auch nicht steht):

because	– *NICHT: becaus*
before	– *NICHT: befor*
decide	– *NICHT: decid*
crocodile	– *NICHT: crocodil*
carbon dioxide	– *NICHT: carbon dioxid*

Practice makes perfect

Use one of the (correct) words above to finish the sentence, as in the example.

He's not coming _______ he has to work tomorrow.
*He's not coming **because** he has to work tomorrow.*

1. *Oh my goodness! Are those _____________ shoes?*
2. *I don't like it, it's the calm ________ the storm.*
3. *The chemical formula for ________________ is* CO_2.
4. *We don't have cable yet, we still have _____________ TV.*
5. *It's time to __________, me or him?*

228. Don't K it – C it!

Wrong *My new laptop has got a defekt.*
Right *My new laptop has got a* ***defect****.*

Erklärung

Es gilt die Faustregel: Steht auf Deutsch ein ‚k', schreibt man auf Englisch ein ‚c'. Beispiele:

*Aspe**k**t – aspe**c**t*
*Defe**k**t – defe**c**t*
***ak**zeptabel – **ac**ceptable*
***K**alendar – **c**alendar*
***K**rokodil – **c**rocodile*
*Kaktus – **c**actus*

Practice makes perfect

Fit one of the words above to the description on the left, as in the example.

A horrible man-eating animal. ***A crocodile***

1. *A thing showing days, months, etc.* ________
2. *A prickly plant.* ________
3. *A malfunction.* ________
4. *Reasonable and tolerable.* ________
5. *View, perspective.* ________

229. How do you feel?

Wrong *Please let me know how you feel on the situation.*
Right *Please let me know how you* ***feel about*** *the situation.*

Erklärung

Viele Verben werden mit Präpositionen kombiniert und bilden sog. **‚phrasal verbs'**. Sie müssen aber richtig eingesetzt werden:

(to) ***fill in***	– *Fill in a tax claim form.*
(to) ***carry on***	– *Don't stop working, carry on.*
(to) ***take off***	– *Take off a garment – The plane takes off at six.*
(to) ***wake up***	– *I usually wake up at about six o'clock.*
(to) ***grow up***	– *I grew up in Manchester.*
(to) ***try on***	– *Would you like to try the jumper on?*
(to) ***throw away***	– *I threw my computer away, it was obsolete.*

Practice makes perfect

Use one of the phrasal verbs above to answer the questions on the left.

What should you do before you buy something in a boutique? ***Try it on.***

1. *How can you get a tax rebate?* ____________
2. *What should you do, if you are too warm?* ____________
3. *Where did you spend your earlier years?* ____________
4. *What do you do with waste paper?* ____________
5. *What would you do, if you found a tramp asleep in your car?* ____________

230. All or every?

Wrong *I have phoned Alan all two days.*
Right *I have phoned Alan* ***every two days****.*

Erklärung

‚all' umfasst alles, das Ganze:
We worked ***all day****.*
We have informed ***all the staff*** *about the pay rises.*
‚every' (‚jeder, jede, jedes') bezieht sich nur auf Teile des Ganzen:
We have informed ***every member of staff*** *about the changes.*
We had to count ***every single item of stock****.*

Practice makes perfect

Use 'all' or 'every' to finish the sentences.

1. *I go to Portugal __________ year to visit my mother.*
2. *He knows _______ the staff by their first names.*
3. *We worked ________ day during the holidays to finish the orders.*
4. *I have to do ________ the housework on my own.*
5. *I have to take the tablets ________ three days.*

231. Same as or same like?

Wrong *Same like you, I hate winter.*
Right *Same as you, I hate winter.*

Erklärung

‚same as' und **‚like'** (beide ‚wie') dürfen nicht im selben Ausdruck verwendet werden – entweder oder:

Same as you*, I'm from England.*

Like you*, I hate maths!*

Practice makes perfect

Use 'same' or 'like' to finish the sentences.

1. *At the end of the day, I'm just _______ you.*
2. *He looks just ______ his father.*
3. *This cake is the _____ as the one we had last week.*
4. *When it comes to money, he's the _______ as his brother. Tight!*
5. *Are you _____ all the others?*

232. Typical spelling mistakes

Wrong *We must protect our enviroment.*
Right *We must protect our **environment**.*

Erklärung

Die englische Rechtschreibung (‚spelling') ist vertrackt, da viele Worte nicht so klingen, wie sie aussehen, und viele stumme Buchstaben vorkommen:
‚would/could/should' haben ein stummes ‚l'
(Aussprache: wud/kud/schud)
‚bomb/plumber/doubt' haben ein stummes ‚b'
(Aussprache: bom/pláma/daut)
‚hour/honest' haben ein stummes ‚h'
(Aussprache: áua/ónest)
Andere Wörter sind einfach schwer zu buchstabieren! Hier sind ein paar Beispiele für Wörter, die häufig falsch geschrieben werden:

definite	*– bestimmt (zweimal ‚i' und ‚e' am Ende)*
embarrassing	*– peinlich (Doppel-r und Doppel-s)*
library	*– Bibliothek (zweimal r)*
personnel	*– Personal (Doppel-n und ‚el' am Ende)*
receipt	*– Quittung (stummes ‚p')*
separate	*– getrennt (zweimal ‚a' und ‚e' am Ende)*

Practice makes perfect

Match a word from above to a description below.

1. *The people who work for a company.* ________________
2. *Awkward.* ________________
3. *Proof of purchase.* ________________
4. *Not together.* ________________
5. *Public book lending facility.* ________________

233. Can't or couldn't?

Wrong *Yesterday I can't sleep.*
Right ***Yesterday I couldn't** sleep.*

Erklärung

Oft wird von vielen Verben die Vergangenheitsform einfach vergessen:

I can't – *I **couldn't***
I must – *I **had to***
I want to – *I **wanted to***
I don't – *I **didn't***
I won't – *I **wouldn't***
she doesn't – *she **didn't***

Practice makes perfect

Use the past tense forms above to write a response to the sentences on the left, as in the example.

Little Sammy started crying when he was told it was his bedtime.
*He **wanted to** stay up longer.*

1. *I offered Bob a drink, but he refused.* ____________________
2. *I was at work until 10 o'clock last night.* ____________________
3. *I was awake all night tossing and turning.* ____________________
4. *He wanted to go out, but I said 'no'.* ____________________
5. *I didn't hear back from Dolly.* ____________________

234. Make or have an experience?

Wrong *We made a lot of great experiences in Australia.*
Right *We **had** a lot of great **experiences** in Australia.*

Erklärung

‚experience' kann gleich auf drei verschiedene Arten genutzt werden kann.
Als Substantiv:
*It was a wonderful **experience**.*
Als Verb:
*I have never **experienced** something like that before.*
Als Adjektiv:
*He is very **experienced**.*
Auf Englisch aber ‚macht' man keine Erfahrungen, man ‚hat' sie!

Practice makes perfect

Use 'experience' in the correct form to finish the sentences.

1. *Do you have any ______________ working with children?*
2. *Are you _______________ in this area?*
3. *He had a lot of strange _____________ in the jungle working with baboons.*
4. *I think it's an _____________ I'll never forget.*
5. *I ________________ a funny sensation when I heard his voice.*

235. Cuisine

Wrong *The English kitchen is not the best in the world.*
Right ***English food/cuisine** is not the best in the world.*

Erklärung

Achtung, Germisch-Alarm! ‚kitchen' ist auf Englisch nur der Raum, nicht die Kochkunst selbst. Andere wichtige Vokabeln zum Thema Essen sind:

menu	*– Speisekarte (NICHT: card, menu card)*
four-course meal	*– Vier-Gänge-Menü (NICHT: menu)*
oven	*– Ofen (aber nur das Gerät zum Braten oder Grillen)*
cooker	*– Herd (oder manchmal auch Kocher, aber nicht der Koch)*
chef	*– Koch, Küchenchef (NICHT: cooker)*

Practice makes perfect

Use the words above to finish the sentences.

1. *If it's not on the ______, they won't do it!*
2. *I think we need a new __________, this one is ancient.*
3. *My compliments to the ________.*
4. *Put the roast in the ________ for two hours.*
5. *We had _________________ for less than €20.*

236. Double letters

Wrong *I only wear sunglases to protect my eyes, not to look cool.*
Right *I only wear* ***sunglasses*** *to protect my eyes, not to look cool.*

Erklärung

Achtung, Rechtschreibsalat! Oft werden auf Englisch doppelte Buchstaben übersehen:

*sate**ll**ite* – *Satellit*
*emba**rr**a**ss**ing* – *peinlich*
*po**ss**e**ss**ions* – *Besitztümer*
*perso**nn**el* – *Personal*
*nece**ss**ary* – *notwendig*
*disa**pp**ointed* – *enttäuscht*
*questio**nn**aire* – *Fragebogen*

Practice makes perfect

Fit one of the words above to the correct definition below, as in the example.

Things that people own. **Possessions**

1. *The people who work for a company.* ____________
2. *A survey.* ____________
3. *Needed.* ____________
4. *Feeling let down.* ____________
5. *Shameful.* ____________

237. One or two words?

Wrong *Have you seen the Lionking musical?*
Right *Have you seen the* ***Lion King musical****?*

Erklärung

Anders als im Deutschen werden Komposita auf Englisch meistens nicht zusammengeschrieben:

Lion King	– *NICHT: Lionking*
football player	– *NICHT: footballplayer*
tennis club	– *NICHT: tennisclub*
washing machine	– *NICHT: washingmachine*
taxi driver	– *NICHT: taxidriver*

Practice makes perfect

Finish the sentences using the correct two-word vocabulary, as in the example.

Jimmy Conners was a great ________________.
Jimmy Conners was a great ***tennis player****.*

1. *Don't wash those clothes by hand, put them in the __________________.*
2. *Have you seen the ___________ musical, it's wonderful!*
3. *Rob got made redundant, he's had to take a job as a _________________.*
4. *We have joined the ____________, now we can play whenever we wish.*
5. *I wanted to be a famous _______________ when I was young.*

238. Sell to or at a price?

Wrong *I sold my car to a really good price.*
Right *I sold my car* ***at/for a really good price****.*

Erklärung

Präpositionen und Preise sind auf Englisch so eine Sache. Achtung vor falschen Freunden! Man verkauft etwas **‚at/for a price'** (zu oder für einen Preis) oder **‚at/for a profit/loss'** (mit Gewinn oder Verlust):

I decided to sell my shares ***at*** *a loss.*
I sold my car ***for*** *a really good price.*

Preise steigen oder fallen **‚to a price'**:

Petrol has gone up ***to*** *€2 a litre.*

Preise steigen oder fallen **‚by a percentage'**:

Prices have increased ***by*** *25 percent.*

Practice makes perfect

Use 'at/for/to' to finish the sentences.

1. *How much did you sell your house _____?*
2. *Did you sell the shares ____ a loss?*
3. *The price of a new notebook has gone down ____ about €500.*
4. *Our share price has fallen ____ 35%.*
5. *We are trading ____ a loss at the moment.*

239. At or on the pavement?

Wrong *We stood at the pavement and waved.*
Right *We stood **on the pavement** and waved.*

Erklärung

Hier ein paar Präpositionen für unterwegs:
*(to) stand **on the pavement***
*(to) live **on** or **in a street***
*(to) live **on the corner** (outdoors)*
*something is **in the corner** (indoors)*
*(to) stand **at a bus stop***
***at the end** of the street*
*(to) be or meet someone **in town***
*(to) go **into town***

Practice makes perfect

Finish the sentences using the correct preposition.

1. *I saw Bob, he was begging _____ the street.*
2. *June's gone _____ town, but she'll be back soon.*
3. *I'll meet you ___ the end of the pedestrian zone.*
4. *You can buy that in that shop ____ the corner.*
5. *Put your bike ____ the corner out of the way.*

240. Why or because?

Wrong *I did it why I was angry.*
Right ***I did it because*** *I was angry.*

Erklärung

Zwei Worte, die leicht verwechselt werden, weil sich ‚why' und ‚weil' so ähnlich sind!
‚why?' heißt ‚warum?':
Why *did you hit him?*
‚because' heißt ‚weil':
Because *he insulted me.*

Practice makes perfect

Use 'why or 'because' to finish the sentences.

1. *He's lost his job _________ the factory closed down.*
2. *Did he tell you ______ he was angry?*
3. _________ *didn't you tell me this before now?*
4. *It's _________ of you we're in this mess.*
5. __________ *don't you apply for the job?*

241. Train or parade?

Wrong *The carnival train went past our house.*
Right *The carnival **parade** went past our house.*

Erklärung

Achtung, falscher Freund! ‚carnival train' ist die wörtliche Übersetzung von ‚Zug' im Sinne von ‚Karnevalsumzug'. Andere Karnevalsvokabeln sind:

carnival procession	– *Festzug*
Rose Monday	– *Rosenmontag*
costume	– *Kostüm*
float	– *Wagen*
wig	– *Perücke*
make-up	– *Schminke*

Practice makes perfect

Match a word from above to a definition below, as in the example.

A day when the big carnival parades go through the major cities.
Rose Monday

1. *A vehicle which makes up part of the parade.* _______________

2. *A fake hairpiece, usually brightly coloured.* _______________

3. *Carnival dress.* _______________

4. *Usually applied to the face in bright colours.* _______________

5. *A long line of vehicles and people.* _______________

242. Guilty for or of?

Wrong *He's guilty for lots of crimes.*
Right *He's **guilty of** lots of crimes.*

Erklärung

Bestimmte Adjektive und Partizipien verlangen bestimmte Präpositionen, z. B. **‚guilty of'**, **‚afraid of'**, **‚exposed to'** oder **‚good at'.** Zum Beispielsatz oben folgt hier ein erweiterter Rechtswortschatz:

innocent of – *unschuldig sein*
accused of – *angeklagt, beschuldigt sein*
acquitted of – *freigesprochen sein*
court case – *Gerichtsverfahren*
lawyer – *Rechtsanwalt*
the defendant – *der Beklagte*
the accused – *der Angeklagte*

Practice makes perfect

Match a word from above to a definition below, as in the example.

A process to determine if someone is innocent or guilty. ***Court case***

1. *Legal representation.* ________________
2. *Not guilty of doing something.* ________________
3. *Proven innocent.* ________________
4. *Suspected of doing something wrong.* ________________
5. *The person who is facing punishment.* ________________

243. When?

Wrong *I am leaving today evening.*
Right *I am leaving **this evening**.*

Erklärung

Zeitangaben werden oft falsch direkt aus dem Deutschen übersetzt:
***This evening** I'm going to the cinema. – (für: heute Abend)*
*I couldn't sleep **last night**. – (für: gestern Nacht, NICHT: this night)*
‚this/next/last/every' benötigen keine Präpositionen:
*Are you going to your French course **this week**? (NICHT: in this week)*
*I'm going to Spain **next Friday**. (NICHT: on next Friday)*
*I went out with Joe **last Saturday**. (NICHT: on last Saturday)*
*Jim plays five-a-side **every Thursday**. (NICHT: on every Thursday)*

Practice makes perfect

Describe the times, as in the example.

After I finish work. ***This evening***

1. *Late yesterday.* ________________
2. *At the end of this week.* ________________
3. *In the middle of next week.* ________________
4. *At the beginning of last week.* ________________
5. *Regularly, on Friday.* ________________

244. In competition to or with?

Wrong *We are in direct competition to them.*
Right *We are in direct **competition with** them.*

Erklärung

Achtung, falscher Freund! Auch wenn man schon weiß, dass man auf Englisch für ‚Konkurrenz' ein anderes Wort benutzt, wird aus ‚Konkurrenz zu' oft ‚competition to'. Richtig ist:

> ***competition with*** *– zu einer anderen Firma oder Person, auch Wettkampf im Sport*
> ***competitor*** *– am gleichen Markt oder im gleichen Rennen*
> ***(to) compete*** *– konkurrieren oder gegen jemanden antreten*

Practice makes perfect

Use 'competition', 'competitor' or 'compete' in the correct form to finish the sentences.

1. *He's one of the main ______________ for the gold medal.*
2. *We decided to pull out of that market, there is too much ______________.*
3. *It's not the winning that's important, it's the ________________.*
4. *Are you ________________ in this year's marathon.*
5. *He always tried to _______________ with his brother.*

245. By the army?

Wrong *I was by the army for 10 years.*
Right *I was **in the army** for 10 years.*

Erklärung

Auf Englisch ist man immer **‚in'** der Armee oder Marine:
*Rob was **in the Royal Air Force**, but he didn't like it.*
*She was **in the Royal Navy**, but now she works in a bank.*
Hinweis: **‚army'** und **‚navy'** werden normalerweise klein geschrieben. **‚Royal Navy'** etc. wird groß geschrieben, weil es ein Eigenname ist.

Practice makes perfect

Write a sentence to describe the person on the right, as in the example.

*Kevin is a pilot. He is **in the air force**.*

1. *Petra's a sailor.* ____________________
2. *Neil's a soldier.* ____________________
3. *Alan's at sea.* ____________________
4. *He's a sergeant major.* ____________________
5. *He's the captain of his own ship.* ____________________

246. Be careful or carefully!

Wrong *It's very slippy outside, be carefully!*
Right *It's very slippy outside, **be careful**!*

Erklärung

Bei Befehl oder Aufforderung wird ‚be' immer von einem Adjektiv gefolgt, nicht von einem Adverb:

> ***Be quiet** – you are making too much noise.*
> ***Be nice** to him, he's just received some bad news.*
> ***Be sensible** – you can't afford to buy that car.*

Practice makes perfect

Use 'be' and an adjective to write a response, as in the example.

I'm just going to the shop to get some milk before mum arrives. ***Be quick!***

1. *Rob wants me to invest in his new company.* ______________
2. *I think I'll build an airraid shelter in my garden.* ______________
3. *The film starts at eight.* ______________
4. *I'm really worried about my interview tomorrow.* ______________
5. *I'm going upstairs to play my new CD.* ______________

247. So or such?

Wrong *He has so a big nose!*
Right *He has **such a** big nose!*

Erklärung

Das deutsche ‚so' zur Verstärkung heißt auch auf Englisch **‚so'** vor einem Adjektiv:

*He is **so arrogant**.*
*She was **so rude**.*

In der Formulierung ‚so ein …' vor einem unbestimmten Artikel (‚a/an') heißt es **‚such'**:

*He had **such a huge** car.*
*They have **such a nice** house.*

Practice makes perfect

Use 'so' or 'such' in the correct way to describe the situation on the left, as in the example.

The check-in queue was a mile long and everyone was shouting.
*It was **so** chaotic.*

1. *I was nearly seasick.* ________________
2. *He's lost his job.* ________________
3. *Our holiday in Spain was fantastic!* ________________
4. *She was very arrogant.* ________________
5. *The party was terrible.* ________________

248. Haircutter?

Wrong *Mum's gone to the haircutter.*
Right *Mum's gone to the **hairdresser**.*

Erklärung

Achtung, falscher Freund! Viele Berufe werden oft falsch übersetzt:

***A hairdresser** cuts your hair.*
***An electrician** installs lights and appliances.*
***A plumber** mends pipes and leaks.*
***A bookkeeper** looks after your financial affairs.*
***A caretaker** is responsible for flats and schools, etc.*
***A nurse** looks after sick people in hospital.*
***A nanny** is usually a young lady who looks after small children.*

Practice makes perfect

Match the person to the job, as in the example.

Fiona works in a salon and doesn't earn much money. **Hairdresser**

1. *Lenny works with figures and numbers.* ______________
2. *Sally works long hours in an old folks' home.* ______________
3. *Dick is responsible for a housing complex.* ______________
4. *Yvonne looks after three young boys.* ______________
5. *Phil is installing a new wiring system in my house.* ______________

249. Look or watch?

Wrong *Do you look a lot of television?*
Right *Do you **watch** a lot of TV?*

Erklärung

‚**(to) look**' beschreibt ein Sehen, das meist von kurzer Dauer ist:
*He **looked out of the window** and saw the birds.*
*Bob **looked up** when we came into the room.*
‚**(to) watch**' bedeutet, dass man sich etwas bewusst für längere Zeit ansieht:
*Did you **watch the game** last night?*
*We **watched a great** film on Sunday.*

Practice makes perfect

Decide if you need 'look' or 'watch' with the following things, as in the example.

A tennis match. ***Watch***

1. *A film on TV.* _______
2. *A documentary.* _______
3. *Birds in the garden.* _______
4. *A mirror.* _______
5. *A basketball game.* _______

250. Fly or flight?

Wrong *When is your fly to Munich?*
Right *When is your* ***flight*** *to Munich?*

Erklärung

Verben nie mit den dazugehörigen Substantiven verwechseln!

It takes 10 hours to ***fly*** *to Cuba, it's a direct* ***flight****.*
We are ***producing*** *more than ever,* ***production*** *has gone up by 30%.*
Our ***advertising*** *agency has just put together a new* ***advertisement*** *for Puma.*
Dick likes designing ***buildings****, his company* ***built*** *the new hospital.*

Practice makes perfect

Complete the chart.

noun	**verb**
negotiation	
	(to) create
	(to) expand
foundation	
manufacturer	

1. Must or had to?

1. *I **have to/must** go to the doctor's tomorrow.*
2. *John **had to** give up his job because of ill health.*
3. *My mum **had to** cook for ten people when she was young.*
4. *I **must** remember to water my plants.*
5. *I **must/have** to go now, bye!*

2. See you

1. *I'll **see you** on Wednesday at seven.*
2. *Sue and Alan won't see **each other** for six months.*
3. *We **hadn't seen** each other since school.*
4. *Have you seen **yourself** in the mirror?*
5. *I'm going on holiday tomorrow, **see you** in a couple of weeks.*

3. Near

1. *I live **near** Jim.*
2. *My new flat is great, there are a lot of shops **nearby**.*
3. *How **near** are you to the school?*
4. *There are quite a few restaurants **near** the office.*
5. *Paul moved because he wanted to be **near** his parents.*

4. By myself or by my own?

1. *I was **by myself/on my own/alone** all night.*
2. *Joe didn't need any help, he did it **himself/by himself**.*
3. *My mum is very lonely, she is always **on her own/by herself/alone**.*
4. *They did it **themselves/on their own**.*
5. *We did it **ourselves/on our own**.*

5. Which or who?

1. *Do you know someone **who** can repair my car?*
2. *John knows someone **who** got sent to prison.*

3. *My mum has a washing machine* ***which*** *is always breaking down.*
4. *I was talking to someone* ***who*** *remembers you from school.*
5. *I have a bike* ***which*** *I don't need.*

6. A friend of you or yours?

1. *Is he a friend of* ***yours****?*
2. *Sue said she's bringing a friend of* ***hers*** *to the party on Friday.*
3. *We bumped into a friend of* ***ours*** *in London.*
4. *A good friend of* ***mine*** *had an accident on Sunday.*
5. *They said he was a friend of* ***theirs****, but I didn't believe them.*

Lösungen

7. Life or live?

1. *I* ***live*** *in Spain.*
2. *Where do you* ***live****?*
3. *This game is coming to you* ***live*** *from Wembley.*
4. *Will there be* ***live*** *music?*
5. *The lifeboat saved many* ***lives****.*

8. Information or an information?

1. *Jill has nice* ***furniture*** *in her office.*
2. *We had great* ***weather*** *on holiday.*
3. *There's* ***information*** *about the meeting on the noticeboard.*
4. *He has a lot of* ***knowledge*** *about Russia.*
5. *I had terrible* ***traffic*** *on the way here.*

9. Make or do?

1. *John is* ***doing*** *his homework.*
2. *Have you* ***done*** *your French homework yet?*
3. *Did you* ***make*** *those candles yourself?*
4. *Who is* ***making*** *so much noise?*
5. *I hope he* ***does*** *the right thing.*

10. Disappointed or disappointing?

1. *I think he is really* ***fascinating****.*
2. *The meeting was really* ***boring****.*
3. *Sometimes my brother's behaviour can be really* ***embarrassing****.*
4. *My job can be very* ***tiring****.*
5. *Are you* ***interested*** *in politics?*

Lösungen

11. Trip or travel?

1. *How many* ***trips*** *to Cuba is that now?*
2. *Diane likes to* ***travel*** *all over the world.*
3. *The* ***travel*** *agent chose a great hotel for us!*
4. *It was a four-hour* ***trip*** *from the airport to the hotel.*
5. *My* ***trip*** *to Rome has been cancelled.*

12. Own or an own?

1. *I'll have* ***my own*** *house by the time I'm 30.*
2. *The dog has got* ***its own*** *basket.*
3. *I can pay for* ***my own*** *drinks, thank you.*
4. *Did he steal that coat? No, it's* ***his own****.*
5. *I can't believe you have* ***your own*** *flat in Spain!*

13. Five year or years?

1. *John has a* ***10-year-old*** *daughter.*
2. *The hotel we stayed at had* ***five stars****.*
3. *He was jailed for* ***10 years****.*
4. *The prisoner was given a* ***five-year*** *sentence.*
5. *It's a* ***10-minut****e drive into the city.*

14. So much or so many?

1. *I have* ***so much*** *to tell you.*
2. *John spends* ***too much*** *money on his car.*

3. *How **much knowledge** do you have about computers?*
4. *I don't know **many people** in this town.*
5. *Her job is just getting **too much** for her.*

15. Spend or donate?

1. *Did you **donate** money to Oxfam again this year?*
2. *Rick **spent** all his bonus on a new car.*
3. *How much did you **spend** on Christmas presents this year?*
4. *He doesn't like **spending** money, he's tight!*
5. *I **donated** €50 to Save the Children last week.*

16. For or since?

1. *I haven't seen him **since** we left school*
2. *I've worked for this company **for** 12 years.*
3. ***Since** when have you been interested in science?*
4. *I've known her **for** over 30 years.*
5. *They have been keeping me waiting **since** three.*

17. Ride, travel or drive?

1. *I like **travelling** by train, it's less stressful than taking the car.*
2. *She **rode/drove** all the way from Frankfurt to Bonn in four hours.*
3. ***Travelling** by taxi is really expensive these days.*
4. *How often do you **ride** your bike to work?*
5. ***Travelling** by public transport is getting more and more expensive.*

18. At, on or in?

1. *I'm meeting Sue **on** Saturday morning.*
2. *Harry always goes for a run **in** the morning.*
3. *My birthday is **in** June.*
4. *My party starts **at** eight.*
5. *They meet in Paris **in** 2001.*

19. Do or commit?

1. *If you* ***commit*** *a crime you could get sent to jail.*
2. *Most murders are* ***committed*** *in the home.*
3. *She couldn't take any more, so she* ***committed*** *suicide.*
4. *He said he didn't do it, but the judge decided he had* ***committed*** *the crime.*
5. *The burglary was* ***committed*** *by two brothers.*

20. Prove or proof?

1. *I know he did it, but I have no* ***proof****.*
2. *He's guilty, but I can't* ***prove*** *it.*
3. *He has* ***proved/proven*** *that he can do the job.*
4. *He admitted it! What more* ***proof*** *do you need?*
5. *You think I'm a liar?* ***Prove*** *it!*

21. The world

1. *After his massage, Phil felt* ***on*** *top of the world.*
2. *This news concerns all the people* ***in/of*** *the world.*
3. *The travel show reports from the four corners* ***of*** *the world.*
4. *After his retirement he wants to travel* ***around*** *the world.*
5. *It's the biggest lake* ***in*** *the world.*

22. Me, myself, I?

1. *I hate* ***myself*** *for being so weak.*
2. *When the job was done, they cleaned* ***themselves*** *in the lake.*
3. *Bob bought* ***himself*** *a new TV.*
4. *Don't worry, I'm sure it will sort* ***itself*** *out soon.*
5. *Sue hurt* ***herself*** *in the fall.*

23. Terrible or terribly? (Possible answers)

1. *Christmas – Christmas is fun. – Christmas is* ***really*** *fun.*
2. *a cream cake – A cream cake is delicious. – A cream cake is* ***especially*** *delicious.*

Lösungen

3. *champagne – Champagne is expensive. – Champagne is* ***terribly*** *expensive.*
4. *a good friend – A good friend is important. – A food friend is* ***extremely*** *important.*
5. *children – Children are sweet. – Children are* ***really*** *sweet.*

Lösungen

24. At or to? (Possible answers)

1. *I was* ***at*** *a really boring party on Saturday.*
2. *Bob fell asleep* ***at*** *the meeting.*
3. *Steve was* ***at*** *a training course yesterday.*
4. *I think she was* ***at*** *the concert.*
5. *I went* ***to*** *Tracey's wedding on Saturday.*

25. Good or well?

1. *I couldn't understand him, his English wasn't very* ***good****.*
2. *Rick did* ***well*** *in his final exams.*
3. *I play piano, but I'm not very* ***good****.*
4. *Her performance was very* ***good****.*
5. *Her job is going* ***well****.*

26. Him or it?

1. *How's the soup? Do you like* ***it****?*
2. *Bob's got a new cat. He's called* ***it/him*** *Fred.*
3. *What's your new boss like? Are you getting on with* ***him****?*
4. *The bus was late. I waited for* ***it*** *for over an hour.*
5. *The dog is barking again. I'm getting really fed up with* ***him/it****!*

27. Hear or listen to?

1. *I often* ***listen to*** *audio books in the car.*
2. *I tried shouting to him, but he couldn't* ***hear*** *me.*
3. *How often do you* ***listen to*** *the radio?*

4. *I like to wake up and **listen to** the sound of the waves crashing onto the beach.*
5. *He **listens to** too much heavy metal!*

28. Normal or normally?

1. *I hate going to the dentist, that's **normal**.*
2. *John **normally** gets up at six.*
3. *He's just a **normal** kind of person.*
4. *I don't **normally** drink so much.*
5. *He **normally** gets a bonus at Christmas.*

Lösungen

29. Tickets or cards?

1. *How many **tickets** do you need for the show?*
2. *I've got a spare **ticket** for the game tonight, would you like to come?*
3. *Oh no! I've got another parking **ticket**.*
4. *Did you send mum and dad a **card** for their anniversary?*
5. *I had to pay a €40 fine because I lost my train **ticket**.*

30. We are/there are (Possible answers)

1. *How many people came to the meeting? **There were** six of us.*
2. ***We are** waiting to hear if we still have jobs.*
3. ***There were** eleven casualties in the crash.*
4. *How many people work in your office? **There are** twelve of us.*
5. ***There were** seven people who wanted the job.*

31. Person or Persons?

1. *How many **people** went to the party?*
2. *He is not a very nice **person**.*
3. *I want every **person** in the company to get a bonus.*
4. *Some **people** don't know when to stop.*
5. *She's not very good with **people**.*

Lösungen

32. Political or politically? (Possible answers)

1. *A safe job – A safe job is* ***extremely important****.*
2. *A riot – A riot is* ***terribly dangerous****.*
3. *A romantic film – A romantic film is* ***really nice****.*
4. *A new-born baby – A new-born baby is* ***absolutely beautiful****.*
5. *A day off – A day off is* ***extremely relaxing****.*

33. Dart or darts

1. *He threw* ***a dart*** *at the dartboard.*
2. *One of my* ***friends*** *is getting married next week.*
3. *Some* ***teachers*** *don't know what they are doing.*
4. *It's last* ***orders****, let me get another round.*
5. *One of my* ***responsibilities*** *at work is to answer the phone.*

34. Invest or investment?

1. *My brother-in-law is in the* ***building*** *trade.*
2. ***Production*** *is down by 25 %.*
3. *Steve has* ***founded*** *his own company.*
4. *We have to* ***negotiate*** *a new contract.*
5. *That's his fourteenth* ***invention****.*

35. Terrible English or a terrible English? (Possible answers)

1. *We need more* ***water*** *for the swimming pool.*
2. *Do we have enough* ***sand****?*
3. *Can I have* ***a pencil****, please?*
4. *John's in* ***a meeting****.*
5. ***Money*** *is the root of all evil.*

36. By or until?

1. *I need those figures* ***by*** *Friday.*
2. *Can you make sure you are here* ***by*** *six?*
3. *We have to leave for the airport* ***by*** *nine.*

4. *I waited* ***until*** *four, then I went home.*
5. *She was gone* ***by*** *the time I got there.*

37. Is or are?

1. *Germans* ***are*** *highly educated.*
2. *Plurals* ***are*** *hard to understand.*
3. *Part-time jobs* ***are*** *badly paid.*
4. *Knowledge* ***is*** *power.*
5. *Weather forecasts* ***are*** *sometimes misleading.*

38. I am or I have been? (Possible answers)

1. *I* ***have been living*** *in my current home for two years.*
2. *I* ***have been living*** *in this country all my life.*
3. *I* ***have been learning*** *English for 10 years.*
4. *I* ***have been reading*** *this book for one hour.*
5. *I* ***have been working*** *for my present company since 2012.*

39. About or not?

1. *We* ***discussed/talked about*** *the situation, but we couldn't find an answer.*
2. *She* ***talked about*** *her new boyfriend all night.*
3. *He's boring, all he* ***talks about*** *is himself.*
4. *Are you* ***discussing/talking about*** *the new budget plans?*
5. *Let's* ***discuss/talk about*** *it when I get home.*

40. Half-time or part-time?

1. *How did you lose? You were winning 3-0 at* ***half-time****.*
2. *The firm doesn't have enough orders, so I'm working* ***part-time*** *at the moment.*
3. ***Part-time*** *jobs are usually badly paid.*
4. *There are five minutes to* ***half-time*** *and I think both teams need a break.*
5. *Looking after children is a* ***full-time*** *job.*

41. Four p.m. or four o'clock p.m.?

1. *We have to be there at* ***four****.*
2. *They are meeting early in the afternoon at* ***two p.m.***
3. *The party went on until* ***four a.m****.*
4. *The concert starts at* ***eight*** *in the evening.*
5. *I've set the alarm for* ***six o'clock****.*

42. A need of or a need for?

1. *There is a huge demand* ***for*** *sports cars at the moment.*
2. *I'm sick and tired* ***of*** *my job.*
3. *He said he was ashamed* ***of*** *himself.*
4. *He shouted at the child, there was no need* ***for*** *that!*
5. *You can be very proud* ***of*** *what you have achieved.*

43. Good in or good at something? (Possible answers)

1. *I'm not very good* ***at*** *languages.*
2. *I'm quite good* ***at*** *cooking.*
3. *I'm terrible* ***at*** *managing my finances.*
4. *I'm not too bad* ***at*** *saving money.*
5. *I'm good* ***at*** *talking in public.*

44. Look on or look at?

1. *Can you* ***look at*** *my car, I think I've got an oil leak.*
2. *We are* ***looking at*** *ways of reducing costs.*
3. ***Look at*** *the state of him!*
4. *He didn't help me out when the trouble started, he just* ***looked on****.*
5. *I'm not sure which one you mean, I'll have a* ***look at*** *it when I get home.*

45. At or on the moment? (Possible answers)

1. ***On*** *my birthday.*
2. ***At*** *Christmas.*
3. ***At*** *Easter.*

4. **On** *New Year's Day.*
5. **At** *night.*

46. Serious or seriously?

1. *No one takes me* ***seriously****.*
2. *Steve is a* ***fascinating*** *man.*
3. *She's a* ***horrible*** *person.*
4. *He spoke* ***horribly*** *to his wife.*
5. *He looks after his money* ***carefully****.*

47. Money in or on the bank?

1. *I think mum is* **in** *the kitchen.*
2. *When you've finished, put the milk back* **in** *the fridge.*
3. *The book you are looking for is* **on** *the kitchen table.*
4. *I always keep my credit card* **in** *my back pocket.*
5. *I saw Bob* **in** *the bank this morning.*

48. At or on Thursday?

1. *I hope it snows* ***at*** *Christmas.*
2. *I have to get up* ***at*** *five o'clock tomorrow.*
3. *Did you go to the party* **on** *New Year's Eve?*
4. *I bumped into Rob in town* **on** *Saturday afternoon.*
5. *We always try to go to church* **on** *Easter Sunday.*

49. On or at my face?

1. *I think she was wearing a watch* **on** *her wrist.*
2. *The baby puts everything* **in** *his mouth.*
3. *Can you see any spots* **on** *my back?*
4. *She has a big hat* **on** *her head.*
5. *The music was so loud, I still have ringing* **in** *my ears.*

Lösungen

50. On or at the sofa?

1. *Sit **at** the table and finish your meal!*
2. *I've been sitting **at** my desk all day.*
3. *Sit **on** the sofa and have a rest.*
4. *I don't like lying **in** bed all day.*
5. *Sit **on** the chair and have a cup of coffee.*

51. Get or have a baby?

1. *Has Julia put on weight or is she **pregnant/expecting**?*
2. *Sue got **pregnant** just after she got married.*
3. *The baby was **due** last week, but nothing's happened yet.*
4. *We are **expecting** our third child in June.*
5. *It won't be long now before we hear **the patter of tiny feet**.*

52. Make or do homework?

1. *Yesterday I **did** my housework.*
2. *Paul is **making** a pizza. It smells good!*
3. *I **did** nothing at the weekend, I was too tired.*
4. *Paul **made** me a cup of tea when I arrived.*
5. *Are you **making** a cake?*

53. Real or really? (Possible answers)

1. *36 ° Celsius is **really** hot.*
2. *A lazy day in bed is **terribly** wasteful.*
3. *A bunch of red roses is **incredibly** romantic.*
4. *A high-scoring football game is **terribly** exciting.*
5. *A cream cake is **extremely** fattening.*

54. Sudden or suddenly?

1. *Paul is a **slow** runner.*
2. *The police arrived **quickly**.*

3. *She wore a* ***beautiful*** *dress last night.*
4. *It started to rain* ***suddenly****.*
5. *It wasn't an* ***easy*** *decision to make.*

55. Condition or conditioning?

1. *My* ***hairdresser*** *is pregnant, I'll have to find a new salon soon.*
2. *Get in touch with our* ***logistics*** *department to arrange delivery.*
3. *My company's* ***headquarters*** *are in the centre of town.*
4. *I believe* ***congratulations*** *are in order, you passed your exam!*
5. *It's freezing in here, please turn the* ***air conditioning*** *off.*

56. At or on your birthday?

1. *I'll take you to lunch* **on** *your birthday.*
2. *I'll see you in the canteen* **at** *lunchtime.*
3. *In England we open our presents* **on** *Christmas Day.*
4. *I'm looking forward to a few days break* **at** *Easter.*
5. *Bob can't come* **on** *Sunday.*

57. Sleeping long?

1. *He's writing* ***on the board****.*
2. *'What is* ***your opinion****?'*
3. *'They are sitting* ***on a bench****.'*
4. *He said I could pay for the treatment* ***in instalments****.'*
5. *I like* ***having a lie-in*** *at the weekend.*

58. Live or living?

1. ***Right.***
2. ***Wrong – I play*** *the guitar quite well.*
3. ***Wrong – I'm reading*** *a good book at the moment.*
4. ***Right.***
5. ***Right.***

59. Will or not? (Possible answers)

1. *Tonight **I'm going** to the cinema.*
2. *Tomorrow morning **I'm going** to work early.*
3. ***I'm going to** Italy on my summer holiday.*
4. *At the weekend **I'm going to** Holland.*
5. *On my next bank holiday **I'm staying** in bed until noon.*

60. Have or not? (Possible answers)

1. *I **have never been** to Spain.*
2. *I **have never ridden** a horse.*
3. *I **have never learned** French.*
4. *I **have tried** Sushi a few times.*
5. *I **have never** bungee-jumped.*

61. Waited or waiting? (Possible answers)

1. *This morning at six I **was having** a shower.*
2. *This time last year I **was doing** a French course.*
3. *Last night at 10 I **was watching** the news.*
4. *This time last week I **was travelling** to Spain.*
5. *Last Saturday at 10 a.m. I **was shopping** in the city.*

62. Become or get?

1. *Did you **get** the report from Alan?*
2. *Who **got** custody of the children?*
3. *It **became** obvious to everyone that he didn't have a clue.*
4. *It is hard to **get** good staff these days.*
5. *Rob applied for the job, but he didn't **get** it.*

63. Introduce or introduction?

Noun	Verb
publishing	***(to) publish***
manufacturing	*(to) manufacture*
fascination	***(to) fascinate***
fantasy	***(to) fantasise***
printing	*(to) print*
production	*(to) produce*
involvement	*(to) involve*

64. Catched or caught?

1. *I **drove** my car to work yesterday.*
2. *I **drank** a lot of beer yesterday.*
3. *I **wrote** 20 e-mails a day.*
4. *I **found** her behaviour strange last week.*
5. *I **had** a lot of backache a few years ago.*

65. Make, do or have a party?

1. *Are you still **doing** a Spanish course?*
2. *Are you **making** fun of me?*
3. *We **had** a lot of fun in the swimming pool.*
4. *Come with us to the show, **have** fun/**it's** fun.*
5. *She only **does** the absolute minimum.*

66. Good weather or a good weather?

1. *Do you need **advice**?*
2. *Do you have **news** about your brother?*
3. *We have old **furniture** in the cellar.*
4. *He can't breathe properly, he needs **oxygen**.*
5. *I don't need **money**.*

67. Recipe or prescription?

1. *They put the photocopier in the* ***corridor*** *outside my office.*
2. *Do you have a good* ***recipe*** *for onion soup?*
3. *Sat I is one of several German TV* ***channels****.*
4. *The garage said they* ***checked*** *the oil but I couldn't prove it.*
5. *The doctor gave me a* ***prescription*** *for painkillers.*

Lösungen

68. Lend or borrow?

1. *He's always* ***borrowing*** *money from his family and friends.*
2. *The bank wouldn't* ***lend*** *me the money to buy a new car.*
3. *Can you* ***lend*** *me €100 until the end of the month?*
4. *I* ***borrowed*** *€50 from Paula, but I paid it back.*
5. *Don't* ***lend*** *him any money, you'll never see it again.*

69. Say or tell me?

1. *He* ***told*** *everyone to go.*
2. *Pete* ***told*** *me you lost your job?*
3. *Did she* ***say*** *goodbye to you?*
4. *Don't* ***tell*** *me, let me guess!*
5. *What did your mum* ***say*** *when you told her?*

70. Bring or take?

1. ***Right.***
2. ***Wrong*** *– Stan* ***took*** *me to the airport on Wednesday.*
3. ***Right.***
4. ***Right.***
5. ***Right.***

71. Lose or loose?

1. *All the lions were roaming* ***loose*** *on the prairie.*
2. *Did you win or* ***lose****?*

3. *He always has a lot of* ***loose*** *change in his coat pockets.*
4. *The buckles on my shoes are* ***loose****.*
5. *In some countries it's important not to* ***lose*** *face.*

72. Stop or stop with? (Possible answers)

1. *I love* ***going*** *shopping.*
2. *I hate* ***doing*** *housework.*
3. *I don't like* ***watching*** *soaps.*
4. *I don't mind* ***washing up****.*
5. *I am trying to stop* ***smoking*** *so much.*

73. Clear up or clean up?

1. *Yes, you can use my new mixer, but make sure you* ***clean up*** *afterwards.*
2. *Why don't you* ***clear up*** *all that mess in your wardrobe?*
3. *I* ***cleared out*** *all the old junk in the shed and sold it at the flea market.*
4. *He went to Vegas and* ***cleaned up****.*
5. *I had to* ***clear up*** *after the kids again.*

74. It gives or there is? (Possible answers)

1. ***There are*** *two parks in our town.*
2. ***There are*** *no hotels.*
3. ***There is*** *one small hospital.*
4. ***There is*** *a private golf course.*
5. ***There is*** *an old town hall.*

75. On or in its place?

1. ***Wrong*** *– Put the dirty laundry* ***in*** *the kitchen.*
2. ***Wrong*** *– That vase is* ***in*** *the wrong place!*
3. ***Wrong*** *– Where's mum? I think she's* ***in*** *the garden.*
4. ***Right****.*
5. ***Wrong*** *– I've hidden the money* ***in*** *a place no one will ever find.*

76. Hard or hardly?

1. *It is really* ***hard*** *to get a university place nowadays.*
2. *Betty is working* ***hard*** *for her exams.*
3. *He puts* ***hardly*** *any effort into his job.*
4. *It is* ***hardly*** *my fault!*
5. *I* ***hardly*** *see Bob since he started his new job.*

77. Desert or dessert?

1. *They were lost in the* ***desert*** *for days.*
2. *Rod's got a sweet tooth, he loves* ***desserts****.*
3. *Is the Gobi the biggest* ***desert*** *in the world?*
4. *What's for* ***dessert****?*
5. *€35? Does that include* ***dessert****?*

78. Sensible or sensitive?

1. *It is a very* ***sensitive*** *situation.*
2. *Be* ***sensible****!*
3. *Negotiations are at a very* ***sensitive*** *stage.*
4. *He's party to a lot of* ***sensitive*** *information.*
5. *She works hard at school, she's a very* ***sensible*** *girl.*

79. Personal or personnel?

1. ***Personnel*** *costs have sky-rocketed over the past year.*
2. *There is no need to get* ***personal****.*
3. *We aren't taking on any* ***personnel*** *at the moment.*
4. *I think she's got a lot of* ***personal*** *problems.*
5. *He always takes everything you say* ***personally****.*

80. Don't or won't? (Possible answers)

1. *She* ***won't*** *have a job by the end of the month.*
2. *He* ***won't*** *be able to help you if you need help.*

3. *He **won't** be long.*
4. *You **won't** see her.*
5. *She **won't** be happy!*

81. Date or appointment?

1. ***An appointment.***
2. ***A date.***
3. ***An appointment.***
4. ***An appointment.***
5. ***A date.***

Lösungen

82. Past or passed? (Possible answers)

1. *In the **past** I lived abroad.*
2. *He **passed** his test.*
3. *It went **past** my house.*
4. *I **passed** the eye test.*
5. *The panic attack has **passed**.*

83. Play or playing? (Possible answers)

1. *She is **cooking**.*
2. *She **cooks** really well.*
3. *He's **fixing** the car.*
4. *She **plays** the piano really well.*
5. *She is **playing** the piano.*

84. Control or check? (Possible answers)

1. *I don't know, I'll **check** it.*
2. *I thought he **controlled** the game well.*
3. *Their mother cannot **control** them.*
4. *She wants to **control** everyone.*
5. *You should have **checked** it earlier.*

85. Briefly or shortly?

1. *I'm going to Portugal on holiday* ***shortly****.*
2. *I lived in North America* ***briefly*** *when I was child.*
3. *It will* ***shortly*** *be time to turn on the Christmas lights.*
4. *We went out together* ***briefly*** *when we were teenagers.*
5. *Harry is due to retire* ***shortly****.*

86. Stationary or stationery?

1. *There's a shop that sells* ***stationery*** *at the end of High Street.*
2. *Put the delivery of* ***stationery*** *in the cupboard.*
3. ***Stationary*** *vehicles littered the motorway after the heavy snowstorm.*
4. *The* ***stationary*** *lorry was loaded with* ***stationery****.*
5. *Our* ***stationery*** *costs are ridiculous.*

87. True or the truth?

1. ***Right.***
2. ***Right.***
3. ***Wrong*** *– Paul insisted that it was a* ***true*** *story.*
4. ***Right.***
5. ***Wrong*** *– During the interrogation they gave him a* ***truth*** *drug.*

88. Take off or put off?

1. *I always* ***put off*** *doing my tax return until the last minute.*
2. *They've* ***put off*** *the budget meeting until the end of the month.*
3. ***Take off*** *your scarf, you must be boiling!*
4. *The plane* ***took off*** *on time.*
5. *Could you* ***take off*** *your shoes, I've just mopped the floor?*

89. High or height?

1. *The bridge was nearly four kilometres* ***long****.*
2. *What is the* ***depth*** *of the water?*

3. *I'm not going on the diving board, it's too* ***high****.*
4. *How much do you* ***weigh****?*
5. *Did you measure the* ***length/width*** *of the garage?*

90. Your or you're?

1. ***You're*** *getting on my nerves!*
2. *Is that* ***your*** *neighbour over there?*
3. *How are* ***your*** *kids?*
4. *That's* ***your*** *problem!*
5. ***You're*** *not going to believe this!*

91. Quite or quiet?

1. *It's not* ***quite*** *what I expected.*
2. *We have* ***quite*** *a lot of work to do on the new house.*
3. *Stop moaning, be* ***quiet****!*
4. *Sam's keeping* ***quiet*** *about her new boyfriend.*
5. *The kids were* ***quite*** *well-behaved today.*

92. Homework or housework?

1. *My Latin* ***homework*** *is impossible.*
2. *Does your maths teacher give you much* ***homework****?*
3. *Dave hates doing* ***housework****, his flat is really dirty.*
4. *Val's doing her* ***housework****, she's wearing rubber gloves.*
5. *I hope he doesn't give us any* ***homework****, I'm away all weekend.*

93. Shade or shadow?

1. *As the sun went down, the trees cast long* ***shadows*** *on the sand.*
2. *It was hot, but we were sitting in the* ***shade*** *of the palm trees.*
3. *The wind was blowing hard and it looked like the* ***shadows*** *were dancing on the lawn.*
4. *I saw a ghostly* ***shadow*** *go past the window.*
5. *Get out of the sun! Come and sit in the* ***shade****.*

94. While or during? (Possible answers)

1. *Phil is working part-time* ***while*** *he is at university.*
2. *Jack was eating* ***while*** *he was working.*
3. *Sally made a mess* ***while*** *she was showering.*
4. *Alan fell asleep* ***during*** *the film.*
5. *The dog smashed a vase* ***while*** *it was running around.*

Lösungen

95. Holiday?

1. ***Right.***
2. ***Wrong*** *– Where did you* ***spend*** *your holidays last year?*
3. ***Right.***
4. ***Wrong*** *– Did you go* ***on*** *holiday last year?*
5. ***Wrong*** *– Where's Bob? Is he* ***on*** *holiday?*

96. Perfect or perfectly?

1. *Roy is a bad driver. – He drives* ***badly****.*
2. *They are a good team. – They play* ***well****.*
3. *He is a* ***wonderful*** *cook. – He cooks wonderfully.*
4. *Steve is a hard worker. – Steve works* ***hard****.*
5. *She is a terrible teacher. – She teaches* ***terribly****.*
6. *Colin is a quick runner. – Colin runs* ***quickly****.*

97. Remind or remember?

1. *Do you* ***remember*** *me?*
2. *Did you* ***remember*** *to switch off the light?*
3. *You always have to* ***remind*** *her to pay her half.*
4. *He* ***reminds*** *me of someone.*
5. *That* ***reminds*** *me, you owe me €20!*

98. Actual or current?

1. *We don't know the* ***current*** *situation, there is a lot of confusion.*
2. *What is your* ***current*** *address?*

3. *I don't **actually** know.*
4. *These are the **actual** clothes he wore in the film.*
5. *We are **currently** considering our options.*

99. Clock or watch?

1. *My alarm **clock** always rings at six.*
2. *Have you got a **stopwatch** which I can borrow?*
3. *The time won't go any quicker just because you keep looking at the **clock** on the wall.*
4. *Ok, let's synchronise our **watches**.*
5. *My parents bought me a lovely bedside **clock** for my birthday.*

Lösungen

100. Same than or same as? (Possible answers)

2. *Wilson & Co have more branches **than** Smith & Son.*
3. *Wilson & Co have the same number of warehouses **as** Smith & Co.*
4. *Wilson & Co have more floor space **than** Smith & Son.*
5. *Smith & Son have a bigger turnover **than** Wilson & Co.*
6. *Wilson & Co have the same number of lorries as Smith & Co.*

101. How expensive?

2. *Hardy is **bigger than** Homestore.*
3. *The Homestore building is **more expensive than** the Hardy store.*
4. *The Homestore product range is **smaller than** the Hardy product range.*
5. *The Hardy building is **older than** the Homestore building.*
6. *The Hardy staff have a **higher** average age **than** the Homestore staff.*

102. In or on the radio/TV?

1. *I listen to music **on** the radio.*
2. *I listen to the news **on** the radio.*
3. *I watch live sport **on** TV.*
4. *I watch films **on** TV.*
5. *I listen to plays **on** the radio.*

Lösungen

103. Article or not?

1. *Bob and Phil are* ***taxi drivers****.*
2. *My dad is* ***a doctor****.*
3. *Sally and Jill are* ***managers****.*
4. *Tim is* ***a teetotaler****.*
5. *Sue and Fey are* ***lifelong friends****.*

104. Like play or playing?

1. *I* ***love eating*** *in nice restaurants.*
2. *I* ***like reading*** *good books.*
3. *I* ***prefer drinking*** *red wine to white wine.*
4. *I* ***hate doing*** *homework.*
5. *I* ***love playing*** *card games.*

105. In or at school?

1. *A 10-year-old girl is* ***at*** *school.*
2. *Someone studying history is* ***at*** *university.*
3. *A young man who wants to a teacher is* ***at*** *teacher training college.*
4. *A child who has just left nursery is* ***at*** *school.*
5. *A girl who has just done her 'A' levels is* ***at*** *grammar school.*

106. Going home or going to home?

1. *I go* ***home****.*
2. *They go* ***home****.*
3. *I'm going* ***home****.*
4. *I'm* ***at home****.*
5. *They go* ***home****.*

107. S or not?

1. *Paul is* ***a good friend*** *of mine.*
2. *Can you wait for* ***two minutes****, please?*

3. *I can't believe my little baby is already **six months** old!*
4. *Did he say '**congratulations**'?*
5. *He was one of the best **teachers** at our school.*

108. In or at an age? (Possible answers)

1. *I left school **at** the age of 18.*
2. *You can legally drink alcohol in my country **at** 18.*
3. *You are eligible to vote in my country **at** 18.*
4. *You can start taking driving lessons **at** 16.*
5. *You can buy cigarettes in this country **at** 16.*

Lösungen

109. Married with or married to?

1. *Jill is **married to** a vicar.*
2. *Dave is **married to** an accountant.*
3. *Key is **married to** a firefighter.*
4. *Alan is **married to** an Arab.*
5. *Susie's **married to** a postman.*

110. On or at Christmas?

1. ***At** night.*
2. ***On** 25th December.*
3. ***On** a Saturday.*
4. ***On** 13th June.*
5. ***On** their birthdays.*

111. From or of?

1. *Their prices start **from** €4000.*
2. *That's a picture **from** my schooldays.*
3. *It's a photo **from** the 1980s.*
4. *They have a value **of** €7000.*
5. *That's a photo **of** my dad.*

112. Do you or would you?

1. ***Do you*** *like tennis?*
2. ***Would you*** *like a game of tennis?*
3. ***Would you*** *like something to eat?*
4. ***Do you*** *feel sick?*
5. ***Do you*** *like Pink Floyd?*

Lösungen

113. Careful or carefully?

1. *Rick said he'd be* ***quiet*** *if he gets home late.*
2. *He answered all the questions* ***truthfully****.*
3. *Can't you be* ***sensible*** *about this?*
4. *I tried to be fair, but it was* ***impossible****.*
5. *I didn't realize it would be so* ***expensive****.*

114. Two weeks? (Possible answers)

1. *As a child I lived in Manchester* ***for 20 years****.*
2. *I last saw my best friend in Paris* ***last year****.*
3. *I watched a DVD* ***two weeks ago****.*
4. *I took my last exam* ***in 1980****.*
5. *I last went to a hot country on holiday* ***in 2011****.*

115. A or an?

1. *Joe is* ***a*** *nice old man.*
2. *I bit into* ***a*** *juicy apple and broke one of my teeth!*
3. *Mum made me* ***an*** *egg and four pieces of toast for breakfast.*
4. *It was* ***a*** *horrible night, the storm was frightening.*
5. *It was* ***a*** *truly exciting experience.*

116. At or on a floor? (Possible answers)

1. *My office is* ***on*** *the second floor.*
2. *My heating system at home is* ***in*** *the cellar.*

3. *Large quantities of wine can be found* ***in*** *a wine cellar.*
4. *Old clothes and toys can be found* ***in*** *the attic.*
5. *An underground car park is usually* ***in*** *the basement.*

117. Interested on or in something?

1. *Al is* ***interested in*** *his work.*
2. *Jake is* ***interested in*** *reading.*
3. *I am not* ***interested in*** *history.*
4. *Sally is* ***interested in*** *extreme sports.*
5. *She isn't* ***interested in*** *me!*

Lösungen

118. Italy or Italian?

Country	Nationality	Sentences (Possible answers)
Wales	***Welsh***	*Rick is from Wales, I think.*
Malta	***Maltese***	*Is that the Maltese cross?*
Burma	*Burmese*	*Where is Burma, actually?*
Greece	*Greek*	*Would you like a Greek salad?*
Peru	***Peruvian***	*What is the capital of Peru?*
Belgium	***Belgian***	*Brussels is in Belgium, isn't it?*
Nicaragua	***Nicaraguan***	*Carlo is Nicaraguan.*
New Zealand	***New Zealander***	*I would love to visit New Zealand.*
Croatia	*Croatian*	*Rob's going to work in Croatia.*
Cameroon	***Cameroonian***	*Have Cameroon qualified for the World Cup finals?*

119. Not or don't?

1. *She* ***doesn't*** *listen.*
2. *He* ***doesn't*** *drive.*
3. *She* ***doesn't*** *like flying.*
4. *She* ***is ignoring*** *me.*
5. *She* ***doesn't*** *like her job.*

120. The birthday?

1. *It's* ***Rob's birthday*** *today.*
2. *It was* ***my birthday*** *yesterday.*
3. *That's* ***Bill's house****.*
4. *That's* ***my daughter's bike****.*
5. *I think that's* ***Rob's wallet****.*

121. Work by or at?

1. ***Wrong*** *– I'm* ***at/with*** *Bolger's.*
2. ***Right.***
3. ***Right.***
4. ***Right.***
5. ***Wrong*** *– I wouldn't like to work* ***with/for*** *him!*

122. For or since? (Possible answers)

1. *I have lived in my current home* ***for*** *23 years.*
2. *I have been reading this book* ***since*** *seven o'clock.*
3. *I've been going to work* ***for*** *23 years.*
4. *I have known my English teacher* ***since*** *last year.*
5. *I have been learning English* ***since*** *I was at school.*

123. Don't or doesn't? (Possible answers)

1. *He* ***doesn't*** *eat healthily.*
2. *They* ***don't*** *get much money.*
3. *He doesn't sleep in the house.*
4. *We* ***don't*** *save money.*
5. *She* ***doesn't*** *speak English very well.*

124. Good or well-organized? (Possible answers)

1. *An inefficient department is* ***badly-run****.*
2. *An intelligent woman is* ***well-educated****.*

3. *A top executive is* ***well-paid****.*
4. *An efficient worker is* ***well-organized****.*
5. *A good book is* ***well-written****.*

125. React on or to? (Possible answers)

1. *She reacted badly* **to** *the news.*
2. *He reacted angrily* **to** *the insults.*
3. *He reacted well* **to** *the situation.*
4. *He reacted generously* **to** *the appeal.*
5. *They reacted* **to** *the invasion with force.*

Lösungen

126. Search or look for?

1. *I saw customs officers* ***searching*** *the guy from America.*
2. *I* ***looked for*** *that book, but I couldn't find it.*
3. *A helicopter was used to* ***search*** *for the missing criminal.*
4. *It's like* ***looking for*** *a needle in a haystack.*
5. *He's* ***looking for*** *a new flat.*

127. Once, twice or three times? (Possible answers)

1. ***Twice****.*
2. *Three or four* ***times*** *a week.*
3. ***Once*** *or* ***twice*** *a year.*
4. ***Once****.*
5. ***Once*** *or* ***twice*** *a month.*

128. All the time or every time?

1. *She drinks* ***all the time****.*
2. ***Every time*** *I see him he's with a different woman.*
3. ***Every time*** *we raise our prices, turnover falls.*
4. *He keeps a gun by his bed* ***all the time****.*
5. *He complains* ***all the time****.*

Lösungen

129. Pension or retirement?

1. ***Pensioner***.
2. ***(to) retire.***
3. ***Pension.***
4. ***Retirement***.
5. ***Rent.***

130. By or on foot?

1. ***On*** *foot.*
2. ***By*** *car.*
3. ***By*** *bus.*
4. ***By*** *plane.*
5. ***On*** *foot.*

131. Crys or cries?

1. *One of his* ***hobbies*** *is fishing.*
2. *She* ***studies*** *history.*
3. *She* ***flies*** *to Rome every summer.*
4. *He bought two* ***copies*** *of my new book.*
5. *She has three small* ***babies***.

132. To or too?

1. *I suppose it's* ***too*** *much to ask?*
2. ***Too*** *many people in our company don't care about their work.*
3. *When we got* ***to*** *the hotel, it was closed.*
4. *Is your sister coming to the party,* ***too****?*
5. ***Too*** *much water was pumped into the system.*

133. The?

1. *We flew out of* ***Gatwick Airport***.
2. *We stayed at* ***the Hilton Hotel***.

3. *We shopped at* ***Macy's****.*
4. *On the way back we had a stopover at* ***Heathrow Airport****.*
5. *But we didn't have time to shop at* ***Harrods****.*

134. This or these?

1. ***This*** *could mean trouble.*
2. ***This*** *pen is useless.*
3. ***This*** *is getting me down.*
4. ***These*** *guys are amazing!*
5. ***This*** *is awful!*

135. A jeans or jeans?

1. ***A pair of*** *shorts.*
2. ***A pair of*** *pyjamas.*
3. ***A pair of*** *tights.*
4. ***A pair of*** *glasses.*
5. ***A pair of*** *swimming trunks.*

136. Capital letters? (1)

1. ***Right.***
2. ***Wrong*** *– We did* ***French*** *at school, I hated it!*
3. ***Right.***
4. ***Right.***
5. ***Wrong*** *– It's your* ***birthday*** *soon, isn't it?*

137. It's a tag, isn't it?

1. *It's getting late,* ***isn't it****?*
2. *You couldn't lend me some money,* ***could you****?*
3. *You're very brown,* ***aren't you****?*
4. *I shouldn't have lost my temper,* ***should I****?*
5. *He'd never met her before,* ***had he****?*

Lösungen

138. Unpolite or impolite?

1. *irrelevant.*
2. *unable.*
3. *unorganized.*
4. *untreated.*
5. *unbelievable.*
6. *unhappy.*
7. *unsure.*
8. *unreasonable.*
9. *irregular.*
10. *unsafe.*

139. Have or had?

1. *I ate sushi last night, I* ***had*** *never* ***eaten*** *it before.*
2. *We rode camels when we were in Egypt, we* ***had*** *never* ***ridden*** *one before.*
3. *I spoke to a Japanese at the airport, I* ***had*** *never* ***spoken*** *to an Asian before.*
4. *I took a painkiller last night, I'****d*** *never* ***taken*** *one before.*
5. *I got picked for the football team today, I'****d*** *never* ***been chosen*** *before.*

140. Auxiliary verb or not?

1. *My brother* ***should drink*** *less.*
2. *My mum* ***cannot cook****.*
3. *Vera* ***might go*** *on holiday in August.*
4. *Wilma* ***should go*** *to bed early.*
5. *My English teacher* ***cannot explain*** *grammar clearly.*

141. Make or take a photo?

1. *I'm* ***making*** *a cake for Billy's birthday.*
2. *I* ***made*** *so many mistakes in my exam, I must be stupid.*
3. *They are* ***making*** *plans for their holiday in Italy in the summer.*
4. *Have you* ***made*** *an appointment at the dentist's yet?*
5. *I have never* ***taken*** *a picture of my car.*

142. Irregular verbs?

Simple present	Simple past	Past participle
hurt	*hurt*	***hurt***
hide	***hid***	***hidden***
bite	***bit***	*bitten*
seek	***sought***	***sought***
let	*let*	***let***

143. Hour or hours?

1. *One and half* ***minutes****.*
2. *Seven* ***weeks****.*
3. *Two* ***years****.*
4. *Two* ***decades****.*
5. *Two* ***centuries****.*

144. Citys or cities?

1. *Little Stevie loves bedtime* ***stories****.*
2. *Badminton is one of my* ***hobbies****.*
3. *I haven't visited many foreign* ***countries****.*
4. *Two little* ***boys*** *threw stones at my cat.*
5. ***Babies*** *are fine, when they are asleep.*

145. Do or doing?

1. *I* ***can't imagine*** *doing it.*
2. *He will* ***continue learning*** *French.*
3. ***Stop doing*** *that!*
4. *I've* ***given up asking*** *him.*
5. *I don't* ***remember saying*** *that.*

146. Some or any?

1. *I've got* ***some*** *books about dinosaurs.*
2. *Natalia hasn't got* ***any*** *friends in Athens.*

Lösungen

3. *I don't think there are* ***any*** *palm trees in Britain.*
4. *Have you got* ***any*** *games for your computer?*
5. *There are* ***some*** *messages for you.*

147. As or than?

1. *New York is much bigger* ***than*** *Paris.*
2. *Is London more expensive* ***than*** *Rome?*
3. *I think Belgium is the same size* ***as*** *Holland.*
4. *The prices in Munich are higher* ***than*** *in Frankfurt.*
5. *Is Sweden* ***as*** *big* ***as*** *Norway?*

148. By or at?

1. *Dad's at the* ***baker's.***
2. *Mum's at the* ***doctor's.***
3. *Dick's at the* ***dentist's.***
4. *Natalia's at her* ***parents'.***
5. *Rick's at his* ***sister's.***

149. Engaged or committed?

1. *Did they invite you to the* ***engagement*** *party?*
2. *His* ***commitment*** *leaves a lot to be desired.*
3. *He's not very* ***committed****, is he?*
4. *Did you get* ***engaged*** *before you got married?*
5. *She doesn't show much* ***commitment.***

150. Floor or corridor?

1. *Put the cartons on the* ***floor*** *in my office.*
2. *He's always standing in the* ***corridor*** *gossiping.*
3. *They've taken the drinks machine out of the* ***corridor.***
4. *There's a big hole in my* ***floor*** *carpet.*
5. *He was standing in the* ***corridor*** *the last time I saw him.*

151. Fast or fastly?

1. *I haven't seen Phil* ***lately****.*
2. *He does* ***hardly*** *any work when the boss is out of the office.*
3. *He was over three hours* ***late*** *and didn't even apologize.*
4. *It was all over very* ***fast****!*
5. *He came very* ***late****.*

Lösungen

152. Mobile or handy?

1. *Kathy's getting a new* ***boss****.*
2. *Fred hates the Chinese* ***cuisine****.*
3. *Candy's a good* ***cook****.*
4. *She doesn't like his* ***style****.*
5. *Tom's* ***cooking****.*

153. Send or broadcast?

1. *Sat 1 are* ***broadcasting*** *the match live.*
2. *The BBC are* ***showing*** *a new series about apes.*
3. ***Send*** *Mary my regards.*
4. *Don't forget to* ***send*** *grandma a birthday card!*
5. *Two people* ***sent*** *Kathy Valentine's cards.*

154. Want or wants?

1. *Some people just do not know what they* ***want****.*
2. *He* ***wants*** *something to eat.*
3. *Harry's not happy at work, he* ***wants*** *more money.*
4. *They said they* ***want*** *to rent the room.*
5. *Somebody* ***wants*** *you on the phone, they didn't give their name.*

155. Proud or pride?

1. *Are you* ***proud*** *of what you've done?*
2. *He had to be very* ***brave*** *to do what he did.*

3. *There was a lot of* ***glamour*** *at the awards ceremony.*
4. *She was very* ***kind*** *to the kids.*
5. *She showed a lot of* ***bitterness*** *towards him after they split up.*

156. Overhours or overtime?

1. *Sally only works* ***part-time****.*
2. *Graham's been working a lot of* ***overtime****.*
3. *Beate's got a* ***full-time*** *job.*
4. *Rick's* ***having/taking*** *a break.*
5. *I usually work* ***overtime****.*

157. Talk or discuss? (Possible answers)

1. *She* ***rambled on*** *and on.*
2. *Rick and Sally* ***argued about*** *the price.*
3. *We* ***discussed*** *the problem.*
4. *Joe* ***ranted on*** *and wouldn't shut up!*
5. *The robber* ***confessed to*** *the crime.*

158. Game or play?

1. *Did you get a part in the school* ***play****?*
2. *Have you ever* ***played*** *for your country?*
3. *He's written three* ***plays*** *but had no success so far.*
4. *To some people life is just a* ***game****.*
5. *He played the* ***game*** *with a protective mask yesterday.*

159. Most or the most? (Possible answers)

1. ***Most*** *of the ice has gone.*
2. *Beijing is the* ***most*** *polluted city in the world.*
3. *Paris is the* ***most*** *popular tourist destination.*
4. ***Most*** *of my friends are away.*
5. ***Most*** *of my teammates are idiots.*

160. His, her or their?

1. *Don't tell him, let him use* ***his*** *brain for once!*
2. ***Their*** *car broke down and they had to walk for miles to get to a garage.*
3. ***His*** *house is always messy, he lives like a pig!*
4. ***His*** *mother left him a lot of money in her will.*
5. *I don't like* ***his/her/their*** *style of management.*

Lösungen

161. Side or page?

1. *On the back* ***page****.*
2. *On the fashion* ***page****.*
3. *On the front* ***page****.*
4. *On the back* ***page****.*
5. *On the letters* ***page****.*

162. Call or call to? (Possible answers)

1. *I* ***call*** *them.*
2. *Six* ***p.m.***
3. *I live* ***near*** *Cologne.*
4. *I would* ***call*** *the police.*
5. *I* ***went*** *home.*

163. Lucky or happy?

1. ***Lucky.***
2. ***Lucky.***
3. ***Lucky.***
4. ***Happy.***
5. ***Happy.***

164. Have or not?

1. *I have* ***ridden*** *a camel many times.*
2. *Last night my brother* ***went*** *to the cinema.*

3. *I **have been** to Ibiza many times.*
4. *We **went** to Italy last year.*
5. *Did you **go** to the concert on Friday?*

165. Decide on or for?

1. *Pat had to go to prison because the jury **decided against** him.*
2. *We **decided to** paint the kitchen blue after all.*
3. *It was a hard decision to make, but we've finally **decided on** Sicily.*
4. *He suddenly **decided to** go.*
5. *We've **decided to** climb Mount Everest.*

166. Devil's circle?

1. *Iris has just had a baby, she's on **maternity leave**.*
2. *She spends the **family allowance** on gin and cigarettes.*
3. *There was a mad rush for the **emergency exit** when the fire broke out.*
4. *He can't get a job, so he drinks because he's depressed, it's **a vicious circle**.*
5. *Mum and dad are celebrating their 50th **wedding anniversary**.*

167. Black and white or white and black?

1. *How those two ever got together I will never know, they are like **chalk and cheese**.*
2. *Do you have any **brothers and sisters**?*
3. *We found a nice **bed & breakfast** down by the lake.*
4. *My plumber friends always tell me that other people's sewage is his **bread and butter**.*
5. *Our company has had its **ups and downs**, but things are ok now.*

168. Note or notice?

1. *I suggest you all make **notes**, I'll only say this once.*
2. *Did you **notice** the looks on all the faces when he came into the room?*
3. *I didn't read the **note** you left for me, what did it say?*

4. *When she **noticed** I was watching her, she started blushing.*
5. *I made a **note**, then forgot all about it.*

169. In former times or I used to? (Possible answers)

1. *I **used to** play football when I was at school.*
2. *I **used to** study hard at university.*
3. *I **didn't use to** be very pessimistic.*
4. *I **used to** live at home, but now I've got my own place.*
5. *I **didn't use** to drink so much alcohol.*

170. Know or knowing him? (Possible answers)

1. *I **hate** him.*
2. *I **regret** that decision.*
3. *I **believe** you.*
4. *It **belongs to** him over there.*
5. *I **have known** her for 24 years.*

171. Neighbour or neighbouring? (Possible answers)

1. *In the **neighbouring** village.*
2. *I **am waiting** for Neil.*
3. *I like **cooking**.*
4. *I think art is very **interesting**.*
5. *They use **air-conditioning**.*

172. Smoke or smoking?

1. *No, I **don't smoke**.*
2. *No, **I'm not smoking** now.*
3. *No, **I don't see** any of the people I was at school with.*
4. *No, **I'm not going** on holiday soon.*
5. *Yes, I **go** on a winter holiday.*

Lösungen

173. Relaxeder? (Possible answers)

1. *Paris is* ***bigger than*** *Bonn.*
2. *A laptop is* ***smaller than*** *a desktop.*
3. *A snack bar is* ***cheaper than*** *a Japanese restaurant.*
4. *Cigars are* ***healthier than*** *cigarettes.*
5. *Jogging is* ***more strenuous than*** *hiking.*

174. Fair priced?

1. *A good book is* ***well-written****.*
2. *A boring book is* ***badly-written****.*
3. *A quiet person is* ***softly-spoken****.*
4. *A brilliant goal is* ***well-taken****.*
5. *An educated man is* ***well-read****.*

175. Ice bears? (Possible answers)

1. *Have you put it* ***on ice****?*
2. *Would you like some* ***iced tea****?*
3. *You will have to* ***de-ice*** *it.*
4. *Did you see the* ***polar bears****?*
5. *Don't worry, we'll soon* ***break the ice****.*

176. At or on the airport?

1. *Bill is* ***at*** *the airport.*
2. *Jan is* ***at*** *a concert.*
3. *Sue and Sam are* ***at*** *the cinema.*
4. *The children are* ***at*** *the seaside.*
5. *Ronnie is* ***at*** *the hairdresser's.*

177. Way or direction?

1. *It's easy, you just have to do it in the right* ***way****.*
2. *Is this the* ***way*** *to the town hall?*

3. *We've been through a bad period, but I think we are going in the right* ***direction*** *now.*
4. *Ask the policeman the* ***way*** *to the M6.*
5. *Left or right? Which* ***way*** *shall we go?*

178. Didn't talk or talked?

1. *Irene* ***doesn't cook*** *hot meals for Nick.*
2. *They* ***don't like*** *each other.*
3. *He really* ***doesn't care*** *about his appearance.*
4. *We* ***don't believe*** *in global warming.*
5. *I* ***don't like*** *your style.*

179. Talking or am talking?

1. *Neil* ***is driving*** *fast.*
2. *Police* ***are searching*** *for the criminals who committed the robbery.*
3. *My band* ***is recording*** *some new songs.*
4. *Helen* ***is baking*** *a cake.*
5. *The mountaineers* ***are climbing*** *Everest.*

180. Look forward to? (Possible answers)

1. *I'm* ***looking forward to finishing*** *work and retiring.*
2. *I'm* ***looking forward to meeting*** *my friends at the weekend.*
3. *I'm* ***looking forward to seeing*** *my family on Friday.*
4. *I'm* ***looking forward to driving*** *my new car.*
5. *I'm* ***looking forward to seeing*** *my children.*

181. Job or work?

1. *Tony's got a* ***job*** *which she really does not like.*
2. *I do all the* ***work*** *and he gets all the credit!*
3. *Your* ***work*** *is not very satisfactory.*
4. *Do you think your* ***job*** *is safe?*
5. *There isn't much* ***work*** *around these days.*

182. The police?

1. *A foreign office official* **is** *giving a press conference this afternoon.*
2. *The policeman* **is** *facing trial for corruption.*
3. *The police* **are** *moving in to stop the rioting.*
4. *The government* **are** *considering their options.*
5. *The army* **are** *deploying more soldiers in Afghanistan.*

Lösungen

183. I will? (Possible answers)

1. *I* **will** *go and buy some.*
2. *I* **will** *print it out for you.*
3. *I* **will** *buy her a nice present.*
4. *I* **will** *go shopping tomorrow.*
5. *I* **will** *pay his bill tomorrow.*

184. Success or successful?

noun	adjective
beauty	***beautiful***
misery	*miserable*
strength	*strong*
violence	***violent***
kindness	*kind*

185. Life?

1. *He always dreamed of* **life** *in another country.*
2. *It's a different way of* **life** *in the outback.*
3. *I'm really worried about the effects of* **global warming**.
4. *Did you go to* **Hyde Park** *when you were in London?*
5. *We are destroying* **nature** *with pollution.*

186. Self or selves?

1. *Jim treated* **himself** *to a new jumper.*
2. *He nearly wet* **himself** *when the dog jumped over the fence.*

3. *If you don't look after* ***yourselves*** *you'll both get sick.*
4. *I'm not very keen on her* ***myself****.*
5. *Leave it, let them do it* ***themselves*** *if they think they are so clever!*

187. Its or it's?

1. ***It's*** *never easy to settle in a new town.*
2. *The petrol station has increased* ***its*** *prices again!*
3. ***It's*** *got nothing to do with you!*
4. ***It's*** *too late now!*
5. *He said* ***it's*** *in the company's own interests.*

Lösungen

188. There or their?

1. ***There*** *are never enough toilets at these events.*
2. *It's* ***their*** *own fault, they wouldn't listen.*
3. ***There*** *is not much we can do about it now.*
4. *She said* ***their*** *bank has agreed to give them a mortgage.*
5. *When* ***their*** *au-pair leaves they'll have big problems.*

189. For or ago? (Possible answers)

1. ***For*** *23 years.*
2. *I met him 23 years* ***ago****.*
3. *40 years* ***ago****.*
4. ***For*** *40 years.*
5. *I left school 35 years* ***ago****.*

190. Was or were?

1. *Pete and Mary* ***were*** *engaged for 11 years before they got married.*
2. *Jenny and I* ***were*** *trapped in a lift for two hours yesterday.*
3. *How long* ***were*** *you at the party for?*
4. *It* ***was*** *not the result I'd been expecting.*
5. *Everyone* ***was*** *shocked when she left him for another woman.*

191. Get up or stand up?

1. *I **dropped** Mum **off** at the airport in plenty of time to get her plane.*
2. *All the people in front of us were **standing up**. We couldn't see a thing.*
3. *He **turned off** the radio and went to bed.*
4. *Can you **turn down** the music? I can't hear myself think.*
5. *Let that alone! **Put** it **down**!*

Lösungen

192. Whose or who's?

1. *I don't know **who's** to blame.*
2. *I wonder **who's** making all that noise.*
3. ***Whose** version do you believe?*
4. *Do you know **who's** putting up the money?*
5. ***Who's** that women standing against the wall?*

193. Waiting or waitting?

1. *Little Jilly loves **feeding** the ducks in the park.*
2. *He **hopped** on one leg all the way down the street.*
3. *Is London **bigger** than Newcastle?*
4. *Look at that lazy dog! **Sunning** himself on the balcony.*
5. *He **reaped** the rewards of his hard work.*

194. Easy or easily? (Possible answers)

1. *I drive **carefully**.*
2. *I talk **quietly**.*
3. *I drink alcohol **regularly**.*
4. *I get angry **quickly**.*
5. *I give blood **annually**.*

195. Take or make?

1. ***Make** food.*
2. ***Take** a break.*

3. ***Take*** *stock.*
4. ***Take*** *it slowly.*
5. ***Make*** *a breakthrough.*

196. Mean or think?

1. *That's not what I* ***meant*** *and you know it!*
2. *He* ***thinks*** *he's the right man for the job, I'm not so sure.*
3. *Do you understand the* ***meaning*** *of the words?*
4. *In my* ***opinion*** *we don't stand a chance!*
5. *He* ***thought*** *he could just walk in here and change everything.*

197. Of or to?

1. *This is the* ***answer to*** *the question.*
2. *That's a* ***matter of*** *fact.*
3. *That's the* ***solution to*** *the problem.*
4. *That's a* ***matter of*** *fact.*
5. *That's a* ***fact of*** *life.*

198. Work?

1. *Did you ring Roy when you got home* ***after*** *work?*
2. *He's not* ***at*** *work today, he's got a day off.*
3. *There's not* ***much*** *work around here since the factory closed down.*
4. *I always need breakfast before I go* ***to*** *work.*
5. *Please don't phone me* ***at*** *work.*

199. By or from?

1. *He was savaged* ***by*** *a vicious dog.*
2. *She said she saw a creature* ***from*** *outer space.*
3. *Have you got any LPs* ***by*** *Fleetwood Mac?*
4. *I think he said he's* ***from*** *Italy.*
5. *He got a postcard* ***from*** *his parents in Spain.*

200. On or in?

1. *He doesn't behave very well for a man* ***in*** *his position.*
2. *Which department are you* ***in****?*
3. *Are we* ***on*** *the same wavelength?*
4. *Are you* ***in/at*** *work at the moment?*
5. *It's a different world* ***at*** *management level.*

201. Is born or was born?

1. *He* ***is*** *Scottish.*
2. *We* ***were*** *in Spain last year.*
3. *I* ***am*** *English.*
4. *They* ***are*** *a couple.*
5. *He* ***was*** *lucky.*

202. Present

1. *I have* ***reserved*** *a hotel room for Jim.*
2. *Please* ***remind*** *me about dad's birthday.*
3. *Champagne is* ***more expensive*** *than sparkling wine.*
4. *My new sports car is really* ***fast****.*
5. *I have to* ***present*** *next year's budget.*

203. Hire or rent?

1. *They've* ***rented*** *a huge villa to celebrate their golden wedding anniversary.*
2. *In Venice we* ***hired*** *a gondola, it was really expensive.*
3. *We* ***hired*** *motorbikes to ride around Sicily.*
4. *Are you* ***renting*** *your flat or did you buy it?*
5. *Jack has to* ***rent*** *a big van to move flat.*

204. Afraid of or about? (Possible answers)

1. *He's* ***worried about*** *losing his job.*
2. *I'm* ***terrified of*** *being made redundant.*

3. *I'm **thinking about** it.*
4. *But I'm **afraid of** spiders!*
5. *I was **afraid of** that.*

205. For or ago? (Possible answers)

1. *Four hours **ago**.*
2. *Two weeks **ago**.*
3. ***For** seven hours.*
4. *About 10 months **ago**.*
5. ***For** 11 years.*

206. Word order (1) (Possible answers)

1. *He **writes poems** really well.*
2. *Have you **seen Val** lately?*
3. *I **exercise regularly**.*
4. *He **passed his test** easily.*
5. *We **played well**.*

207. Word order (2) (Possible answers)

1. *He **always stays** at a hotel.*
2. *I **usually help** Helen.*
3. *He **doesn't always need** treatment.*
4. *They **couldn't always reach** the final.*
5. *He **doesn't usually play** basketball.*

208. Hand or side?

1. *The **electrician** put the plugs on the wrong wall.*
2. *He **donated** most of the money he won to charity.*
3. *He was so **happy**, he started crying.*
4. *Where did you **get** that nice suntan?*
5. *There's nothing on the **menu** I fancy.*

Lösungen

209. Wore or weared?

1. *He **broke** every toy he **got**.*
2. *He **dreamt** about sheep.*
3. *He **slept** like a baby.*
4. *The wind **blew** hard.*
5. *He **rang** the doorbell.*

210. Eastern or Easter? (Possible answers)

1. ***On** Saturday.*
2. ***At** six o'clock.*
3. ***On** my birthday.*
4. ***At** Christmas.*
5. ***At** Easter.*

211. Children or childrens?

1. *The dentist had to give me a filling in one of my **teeth**.*
2. *He follows her around like a **sheep**.*
3. *He wears clothes that would look more suitable on **women**.*
4. *I think we've got **mice** in the cellar.*
5. *Not all **men** are macho.*

212. Build or build up?

1. *He's **built up** a loyal following over the last 25 years.*
2. *The traffic is **building up**. It'll take hours to get home.*
3. *This particular model was **built** in 1934.*
4. *They are **building** a huge housing estate on the edge of town.*
5. *They had to completely re-**build** the village after the hurricane.*

213. Used to doing something? (Possible answers)

1. *He's **used to** it.*
2. *He **used to** see them a lot.*

3. *He's **used to working** with fumes.*
4. *She **used to live** here.*
5. *He's **used to giving** her a lift.*

214. In or on the countryside? (Possible answers)

1. *I don't live **in** Germany.*
2. *I live **in** a house.*
3. *I live **in** a small village.*
4. *I live **in** the countryside.*
5. *I live **in** Europe.*

215. Hours (Possible answers)

1. *I **spend days walking** in the hills.*
2. *I **spend weeks working** on projects at work.*
3. *I **spend months training** new staff.*
4. *I **spend years saving** money.*
5. *I **spend ages waiting** for buses.*

216. Apprenticeship

1. *He **did** an apprenticeship as a plumber, then got a job driving a taxi.*
2. *Has she **done** the shopping?*
3. *They **did** a lot of advertising for the new product.*
4. *We've **done** our best, it's up to you now.*
5. *Can you **do** me a favour?*

217. In or on average? (Possible answers)

1. ***On average** I go shopping once a week.*
2. *I **normally** go to bed at about 11 o'clock.*
3. ***As a rule** I don't smoke in the house.*
4. *I **typically** go on holiday in June or July.*
5. *I **usually** get up at six o'clock.*

218. Affect of effect?

1. *Were you **affected** by the wave of redundancies?*
2. *There will be a knock-on **effect** of the local mill closing.*
3. *I think this recession **affects** all of us.*
4. *What were the after **effects** of the riots?*
5. *Try not to let the crowd **affect** your concentration.*

219. There or they're?

1. ***There** might be a surprise in store for you!*
2. ***They're** not taking on any more staff at the moment.*
3. *I think I'll build my house over **there**.*
4. *When **they're** on holiday, they always lie on the beach.*
5. ***They're** not telling the truth.*

220. Toys or toy's?

1. *Ron has bought 20 pounds of food for his white mice.*
2. *Dad found a **woman's** handbag on the train yesterday.*
3. *Those scissors are really sharp, be careful!*
4. *I need a new pair of trousers for work.*
5. *She went to a **girls**' school.*

221. Then or than?

1. *Her new boyfriend is much older **than** I expected.*
2. *It's a lousy job, but it's better **than** nothing.*
3. ***Then** we found out that the money had not been paid into our account.*
4. *Dad's doing ok, his temperature is lower **than** it was yesterday.*
5. *I think he's bit off more **than** he can chew!*

222. Compliments or complements?

1. *If that's a **compliment**, I wouldn't like to hear her insults.*
2. *Do you really thing baked beans are the right kind of **complement** to salmon?*

3. ***Compliments** of the season to you all.*
4. *My mother sends her **compliments**.*
5. *He **complimented** me on my new haircut.*

223. Advice or advise?

1. *Maybe you should go the Citizen's **Advice** Bureau?*
2. *My brother could **advise** you, he's a lawyer.*
3. *I'm looking for some sound financial **advice**.*
4. *It's my job as your bank manager to **advise** you.*
5. *If you'd have listened to your parents' **advice**, this would never have happened.*

Lösungen

224. Cancelled or delayed?

1. ***Cancelled.***
2. ***Delayed.***
3. ***Delayed.***
4. ***Delayed.***
5. ***Cancelled.***

225. Make a trip? (Possible answers)

1. *He **went on** a sight-seeing tour.*
2. *She **went on** a boat trip.*
3. *He **took** a long holiday.*
4. *He **went on** a donkey ride.*
5. *She **took** a walking holiday.*

226. Capital letters? (2)

1. *Can you put it all in an **e**-mail?*
2. *The **h**otel was **g**reat.*
3. *Bruno sends his **l**ove.*
4. *I bought the new **R**od Stewart **r**ecord. It's great!*
5. *Jill stayed at the Hilton for **t**wo **n**ights.*

Lösungen

227. Don't forget the e!

1. *Oh my goodness! Are those* ***crocodile*** *shoes?*
2. *I don't like it, it's the calm* ***before*** *the storm.*
3. *The chemical formula for* ***carbon dioxide*** *is* CO_2.
4. *We don't have cable yet, we still have* ***satellite*** *TV.*
5. *It's time to* ***decide****, me or him?*

228. Don't K it – C it!

1. ***A calendar.***
2. ***A cactus.***
3. ***A defect.***
4. ***Acceptable.***
5. ***An aspect.***

229. How do you feel? (Possible answers)

1. ***Fill in*** *a form.*
2. ***Take off*** *your jumper.*
3. *I* ***grew up*** *in Berlin.*
4. ***Throw*** *it* ***away****.*
5. ***Wake*** *him* ***up****.*

230. All or every?

1. *I go to Portugal* ***every*** *year to visit my mother.*
2. *He knows* ***all*** *the staff by their first names.*
3. *We worked* ***all/every*** *day during the holidays to finish the orders.*
4. *I have to do* ***all*** *the housework on my own.*
5. *I have to take the tablets* ***every*** *three days.*

231. Same as or same like?

1. *At the end of the day, I'm just* ***like*** *you.*
2. *He looks just* ***like*** *his father.*

3. *This cake is the* ***same*** *as the one we had last week.*

4. *When it comes to money, he's the* ***same*** *as his brother. Tight!*

5. *Are you* ***like*** *all the others?*

232. Typical spelling mistakes

1. ***Personnel.***
2. ***Embarrassing.***
3. ***Receipt.***
4. ***Separate.***
5. ***Library.***

Lösungen

233. Can't or couldn't? (Possible answers)

1. *He* ***didn't*** *want a drink.*
2. *I* ***had to*** *do overtime.*
3. *I* ***couldn't*** *sleep.*
4. *I* ***wouldn't*** *let him go out.*
5. *She* ***didn't*** *reply to my letter.*

234. Make or have an experience?

1. *Do you have any* ***experience*** *working with children?*
2. *Are you* ***experienced*** *in this area?*
3. *He had a lot of strange* ***experiences*** *in the jungle working with baboons.*
4. *I think it's an* ***experience*** *I'll never forget.*
5. *I* ***experienced*** *a funny sensation when I heard his voice.*

235. Cuisine

1. *If it's not on the* ***menu****, they won't do it!*
2. *I think we need a new* ***cooker/oven****, this one is ancient.*
3. *My compliments to the* ***chef****.*
4. *Put the roast in the* ***oven*** *for two hours.*
5. *We had* ***a four-course meal*** *for less than €20.*

236. Double letters

1. ***Personnel.***
2. ***Questionnaire.***
3. ***Necessary.***
4. ***Disappointed.***
5. ***Embarrassing.***

237. One or two words?

1. *Don't wash those clothes by hand, put them in the* ***washing machine****.*
2. *Have you seen the* ***Lion King*** *musical, it's wonderful!*
3. *Rob got made redundant, he's had to take a job as a* ***taxi driver****.*
4. *We have joined the* ***tennis club****, now we can play whenever we wish.*
5. *I wanted to be a famous* ***football player*** *when I was young.*

238. Sell to or at a price?

1. *How much did you sell your house* ***for****?*
2. *Did you sell the shares* ***at*** *a loss?*
3. *The price of a new notebook has gone down* ***to*** *about € 500.*
4. *Our share price has fallen* ***by*** *35 %.*
5. *We are trading* ***at*** *a loss at the moment.*

239. At or on the pavement?

1. *I saw Bob, he was begging* ***on*** *the street.*
2. *June's gone* ***into*** *town, but she'll be back soon.*
3. *I'll meet you* ***at*** *the end of the pedestrian zone.*
4. *You can buy that in that shop* ***on*** *the corner.*
5. *Put your bike* ***in*** *the corner out of the way.*

240. Why or because?

1. *He's lost his job* ***because*** *the factory closed down.*
2. *Did he tell you* ***why*** *he was angry?*

3. ***Why** didn't you tell me this before now?*
4. *It's **because** of you we're in this mess.*
5. ***Why** don't you apply for the job?*

241. Train or parade?

1. ***A float.***
2. ***A wig.***
3. ***A costume.***
4. ***Make-up.***
5. ***Carnival parade.***

Lösungen

242. Guilty for or of?

1. ***Lawyer.***
2. ***Innocent.***
3. ***Not guilty.***
4. ***Accused.***
5. ***Defendant.***

243. When?

1. ***Last** night.*
2. ***This** Friday.*
3. ***Next** Wednesday.*
4. ***Last** Monday.*
5. ***Every** Friday.*

244. In competition to or with?

1. *He's one of the main **competitors** for the gold medal.*
2. *We decided to pull out of that market, there is too much **competition**.*
3. *It's not the winning that's important, it's the **competing**.*
4. *Are you **competing** in this year's marathon?*
5. *He always tried to **compete** with his brother.*

245. By the army?

1. *She's **in** the navy.*
2. *He's **in** the army.*
3. *He's **in** the Royal Navy.*
4. *He's **in** the army.*
5. *He's **in** the navy.*

246. Be careful or carefully! (Possible answers)

1. *Be **careful**!*
2. *You must be **mad**!*
3. *Don't be **late**.*
4. *Don't be **nervous**.*
5. *Don't be too **loud**.*

247. So or such? (Possible answers)

1. *The sea was **so rough**.*
2. *He's **so upset** about it.*
3. *It was **so relaxing**.*
4. *She's **such a** cow!*
5. *It was **so boring**.*

248. Haircutter?

1. ***Bookkeeper.***
2. ***Nurse.***
3. ***Caretaker.***
4. ***Nanny.***
5. ***Electrician.***

249. Look or watch?

1. ***Watch.***
2. ***Watch.***

3. ***Watch/look (at).***
4. ***Look (in).***
5. ***Watch.***

250. Fly or flight?

noun	**verb**
negotiation	***(to) negotiate***
creation	*(to) create*
expansio*n*	*(to) expand*
foundation	***(to) found***
manufacturer	***(to) manufacture***